Capitalist Economics

Capitalist Economics

SAMUEL A. CHAMBERS

OXFORD
UNIVERSITY PRESS

Oxford University Press is a department of the University of Oxford. It furthers the University's objective of excellence in research, scholarship, and education by publishing worldwide. Oxford is a registered trade mark of Oxford University Press in the UK and certain other countries.

Published in the United States of America by Oxford University Press
198 Madison Avenue, New York, NY 10016, United States of America.

CIP data is on file at Library of Congress
ISBN 978-0-19-755689-4 (pbk.)
ISBN 978-0-19-755688-7 (hbk.)

DOI: 10.1093/oso/9780197556887.001.0001

1 3 5 7 9 8 6 4 2

Paperback printed by Marquis, Canada
Hardback printed by Bridgeport National Bindery, Inc., United States of America

To my students,
who have taught me more than they know

Contents

Contents

Preface

We are currently living through a period of history that calls into question and places at stake the very meaning of both "economics" and "capitalism." This has happened before.

From the beginning of World War I (1914) to the end of World War II (1945), economics was remade by history itself. What John Maynard Keynes called the "classical school" of economics—as taught to him by Alfred Marshall, the author of the first great economics textbook—rested on the principle that markets were naturally occurring, self-regulating, and always moving *toward* an equilibrium. Economics could therefore not directly *create* political conflict, and economic downturns should be dealt with mainly through patience. While Keynes himself famously challenged the entire classical paradigm in his *General Theory* (1936), far and away the most important work of economics published in the twentieth century, the most damning critique of classical economics came not from Keynes but from the events of history—two global wars and one global economic depression.

By the end of World War II, Marshall's *Principles of Economics* (1890) was not just out of date at more than a half century of age, it was completely out of touch and inappropriate for a world that had been entirely transformed. In both Britain and the United States, Keynes's utterly unorthodox approaches to monetary policy (including inflation/deflation), taxation, debt, trade, and economic growth had effectively transformed economic policy, and by any measures such policies had been a resounding success. When American President Franklin Delano Roosevelt first experimented with Keynesian ideas, as a desperate measure to bring America out of the Depression, the results were impressive: GDP grew at 10.8, 8.9, and 12.9 percent in 1934, 1935, and 1936, respectively. When, at the start of his second term in office, Roosevelt switched course, cut spending, and balanced the budget, the US economy fell back into depression. And finally, when the war economy forced a return to the Keynesian playbook, the United States experienced truly staggering growth rates—exceeding 17 percent each year from 1941 to 1943.

By 1945 top economics departments in the United States were filled with young scholars who had both learned and implemented (through direct policymaking) the new economic ideas of the day. The time was ripe for a new textbook that could teach these ideas to the largest generation of students (expanded massively by the GI Bill) ever to attend college. And no one thought for a moment that Keynes's great book could serve as such an introduction: the exposition of ideas in that text was obtuse and impenetrable—clear as mud.

In 1947, an assistant professor at Stanford University was the first to act. At the age of 36, Lorie Tarshis was still quite young for an academic, but like many of his generation he had already lived a life full of experiences. A Canadian by birth, Tarshis had gone from the University of Toronto to study with Keynes at Cambridge University, where he completed an MA and a PhD, before moving to the United States to teach at Tufts University. During World War II he first worked for Roosevelt's War Production Board and then served as an analyst for the US Army Air Forces. After the war he took up a post at Stanford and quickly began work on the much-needed textbook, which he published a year later.

Read today, *Elements of Economics* looks like the typical textbook: long (700-plus pages), dry, and filled with aggregate economic numbers and plenty of the basic charts and graphs that had been the stuff of economics since Marshall. Nothing about the book stands out. It begins with the usual proclamations about the need to study economics as a scientist would (and not as a philosopher or theologian would), and it devotes a very early chapter to underscoring the essential importance of the capitalist firm: "the presence of the private, independent business firm is the most important feature of a capitalist economy" (Tarshis 1947: 28). Tarshis goes on to spell out that such firms seek to maximize profits, and he insists that these are not "act[s] of villainy" (Tarshis 1947: 30). A careful reader might notice that the book spends significant time discussing the role of government spending in a national economy, and that it devotes an entire section to money, banking, and the central banking system, but otherwise it seems like a standard textbook.

The book was important not because it was unorthodox but surely because it met an extreme of pent-up demand, as economics departments all across the country needed an introductory text to teach their growing student bodies. Upon its appearance the book quickly emerged as something of "an academic publishing hit": "when the book came out, professors at Brown, Middlebury, Yale, and other universities eagerly picked it up. *Elements of Economics* went through about ten thousand copies in just a few months" (Carter 2020: 375). This is an enormous success by academic publishing standards and portended a great future for both Tarshis and his textbook: once a text becomes a "standard" or a set text for introductory courses, it tends to gain inertia—as instructors return to the text they know well, and publishers therefore bring out updated editions to maintain sales.

Yet today none but a few economic historians have ever heard of Lorie Tarshis, and no one since the 1940s has read *Elements of Economics*. What happened?

The story proves slightly complicated, but it is first and last a political story. Almost immediately upon publication of Tarshis's text, Merwin Hart, a corporate lawyer with no economic training, led a proto-McCarthyist campaign against Tarshis and his book. It began with a scathing review explicitly calling the book "pre-Christian" Marxist propaganda and asserting that the book was "part of a dangerous subversive plot." Hart started what today we would call an "astroturf" campaign, an effort to drum up the appearance of a grassroots movement against the book. He sent a form letter to newspapers and to university administrators and trustees all across the country; it claimed that the choice was between freedom and private enterprise, on the one hand, and "a Socialism like that of Britain . . . [itself only] a transitory stop on the road to State Absolutism such as that of Russia," on the other. The campaign to convince local newspapers to editorialize against the book proved highly effective, with many suggesting that the book was an obvious effort to teach Marxism. In turn, the pressure on university administrations succeeded as well, with some actively removing the book because of its putative ideology but most merely wishing to avoid controversy. Tarshis's publisher dropped the book in less than a year. While Tarshis had a long career at Stanford and then at universities back in his home country of Canada, he never made a mark on economics, but instead became a footnote in economic history. And aside from the handful who happened to take introductory economics courses in 1947, very few students read his textbook.

At the very moment that Tarshis's publisher was abandoning his book, Paul Samuelson published his own textbook, which perfectly "slipped in to fill the teaching void left by the Tarshis text" (Carter 2020: 377). Samuelson's parsimoniously named *Economics* (1948) would go on to become not just the most enduring, widely read, and financially successful economics textbook of all time, but arguably the single most successful textbook in any field. Over a span of four decades, Samuelson solo-authored 12 editions of the book; seven more editions (19 in total) were then coauthored by Samuelson and William Nordhaus; the 2009 edition of the book remains in print and widely used in the classroom today. Since 1961, each and every edition of *Economics* has sold a minimum of 300,000 copies, with total sales surpassing four million. Paul Samuelson is described today on his Wikipedia page as "the most influential economist of the later twentieth century." While his research surely contributes to that status, Samuelson himself emphasized the importance of the textbook. In a famous, though perhaps apocryphal, quote, he boasted, "I don't care who writes a nation's laws—or crafts its advanced treaties—if I can write its economics textbooks" (quoted in Carter 2020: 378).

◍◍◍◍

This is not a history book; it is an introduction to political economy. So why does it begin with a 75-year-old story? First, the tale of the Tarshis and Samuelson textbooks powerfully illustrates that the production and dissemination of knowledge cannot be sealed off from political relations of power and authority. Knowledge itself always includes a relation to history—what we study will always be historical in that it remains situated within history. This does not taint all knowledge or turn it into bias. To the contrary, the recognition that no knowledge is "pure," that history cannot be transcended, gives us more, not less, reason to aim for a certain "objectivity" and disinterestedness in our pursuit of knowledge. There remains a wide chasm separating the search for understanding and explanation, on the one hand, from an instrumental use of information to support an already established position, on the other. Nonetheless, we search for knowledge (for truth, even) not from a place beyond history but precisely from our actual location within history.

Second, more simply and more fundamentally, we learn from this story that *economics is never not political*. There is no way to study economic forces and relations as existing separately from political forces and relations. This is not only because any particular historical example of an economic event will be bound up with politics but also because there is no economic domain outside of other domains (social, cultural, political) and because there are no economic forces except those deeply entangled with political forces. To boil this point down we can put it this way: we cannot study "economics"; we can only ever study *political economy*.

This book provides an introduction to that field of study and to concrete phenomena of the world in which we live. Importantly, this field is not itself an academic discipline. Indeed, the name "political economy" seems to combine simply (or perhaps contradictorily) two discrete, separate disciplines: economics and political science. You can get a university degree in something called "political economy," but if you do it will be explicitly marked as interdisciplinary—and therefore very different from a degree in economics. As established academic disciplines, tens of thousands of students major in economics and political science every year, and both disciplines are overflowing with introductory texts and textbooks. However, if you search for an introduction to "political economy," your search will only turn up selections from the history of economic thought or specialist texts that describe narrower fields that lie within economics or political science, especially texts in international political economy (a field itself built on mainstream economics). What does it mean, then, to study political economy at a more basic, more fundamentally introductory level?

To answer that question we first have to consider the relation between politics and economics. In particular, we need to address two standard, guiding assumptions: that political science analyzes and explains the discrete domain of politics, while economics does the same with "the economy." These assumptions combine to underscore the claim that politics and economics are different domains, constituted by different elements and forces, and that each separate discipline devotes itself to the task of making sense of its own specified area. Many economics textbooks are explicit about this point; they will go out of their way to *distinguish* economics from politics and to explain to students that economics as a scientific endeavor can and must be carried out separately from politics. Politics textbooks are less likely to *exclude* economics, but they will tacitly assume that economics can be left to the economists. At the same time, most textbooks in either field will affirm that they offer an examination of objective facts about their disciplines, and that *actual politics* (partisan conflict, collective struggle, and social strife) remains outside the text. In other words, textbooks are not themselves political. As we demonstrated previously, these claims prove completely untenable. Textbooks are shaped by the politics of their time, and occasionally—as with the case of Tarshis and Samuelson—they are heavily stamped and decisively marked by that politics.

Lost in history alongside Lorie Tarshis is the story of the first edition of Samuelson's textbook, which was also subject to a version of the same political attack that took down Tarshis. William Buckley, in the book that made his career as a conservative thinker, attacked Samuelson's book right alongside Tarshis's. The difference was that Buckley's attack came later (1951) and was not combined with a coordinated political campaign. Moreover, Samuelson's book was easier to defend because it offered a compromise between "classical economics" and the thought of Keynes. But most importantly, both Samuelson and his publisher directly and vigorously fought back against attacks on the book (Carter 2020: 377). Were it not for the fact that they won this political battle, the most successful economics textbook of all time might well be buried in history alongside Tarshis's *Elements of Economics*.

The goal of this book is to offer an introduction to political economy in the form of a broad study of capitalist economics. Our main focus will be *economic* forces and relations, but we will study them without ever pretending that they are universal or timeless (that they could somehow be purely "natural"). One of our aims will be to see that specific types of economic forces only come into existence after (and based on) social, political, and cultural changes. Another will be to grasp that economic forces never operate in a vacuum: they are always competing with or complementing those other forces—forces of law, forces of society, and even forces of nature.

This is not a "textbook" as we usually understand that term. It has fewer chapters, fewer pages, fewer graphs and charts, and no study guides, built-in quizzes, or any of the other "options and features" that usually constitute textbooks today and help to justify their exorbitant prices. But it *is* an introductory text designed to help both students and general readers make sense of something quite fundamental to all of our lives: capitalist economics.

And while the historical contexts prove quite distinct, it's probably fair to say that I came to write this book for many of the same reasons that Tarshis and Samuelson wrote theirs. Like them (and like all of you) I have recently lived through an extraordinary historical period in which, to use a phrase that Keynes himself coined, the "conventional wisdom" in both economics and politics has been completely shaken. Like them, I have spent about a decade and a half studying, learning, and exploring both new and old ideas that, when combined, can provide a sharper and more useful picture of both political economy in general and capitalist economics in particular. As was the case for Tarshis and Samuelson in their time, the current disciplinary textbooks are no longer fit for purpose.

We need to start over, but we do not need to start from scratch. This book draws from a wide range of sources in the history of economic thought, political theory, history and anthropology, synthesizing them in a simpler, clearer overview of capitalist economics. With the goals of clarity, parsimony, and readability paramount, the main body of the text does not cite even a fraction of those sources. Readers who just want to understand the ideas can focus their attention here. Readers who want to know where the ideas come from, to engage with them more deeply or at higher levels of sophistication, or to explore avenues of investigation of their own should spend time consulting the Sources and Further Reading section at the end of the book.

The implied reader of the book is . . . anyone and everyone. No specific prior knowledge is presumed. I worked out the ideas of the book over 14 years of teaching at both the undergraduate and graduate level at Johns Hopkins University. Early drafts of the manuscript served as the set text for my introductory courses in both Spring 2020 and Spring 2021, so the book can clearly fulfill the main textbook function in an introduction to political economy course. All or part of it could also be assigned in more advanced undergraduate or graduate courses where the instructor wants to expose students to some general ideas of political economy or to give them a functional working understanding of capitalist economics, while avoiding the disciplinary entanglements of the models that form the basis of neoclassical economics. Moreover, and I cannot emphasize this enough, although the book is written by an academic and I think it has a role to play within college and university curriculums, this is not an academic text. This book is also, and in a way primarily, written for the following: anyone who has found themselves wanting to be able to make better sense of what's going on with "the economy" today; everyone who reads the business or financial pages of the newspaper and finds their explanations wanting; and anyone who just doesn't buy the idea that economic growth, or the fluctuations of stock and bond prices, is somehow just a "natural" reflection of the emotion of "investors."

The foundational research work for this book was not undertaken with the intention of producing a book like this. I started out on this path of exploration precisely because I was not satisfied with newspapers', textbooks', or economists' explanations of the great financial crisis of 2008. I soon learned enough to know that many of the standard newspaper stories on political economy were often saying little at all, and sometimes just repeating falsehoods. This book does not contain all the answers, for the very good reason that these are complicated, dynamic, and deeply challenging problems. (For example, any *simple* explanation of something like bond yield curves is a *bad* explanation.)

The book *does* provide a solid grounding and clear framework for seeking such answers, for building rich, substantive responses to the questions and problems we face today. It aims to give readers a much firmer grasp of the fundamental relation between politics and economics. First, it locates economic forces and relations in history; specifically, it explains that capitalism is a unique economic form that first

emerged at a particular time and place in history. Then, from this basis
the book explores fundamental economic relations and forces in great
depth, providing the reader with both a deeper understanding of how
these forces operate and a set of tools they can use to make sense of
concrete phenomena.

Introduction: What Is Economics?

Everyone knows that the noun "economics" names an academic discipline in the social sciences, as well as a general profession. Economics studies individual choices in relation to the efficient allocation of scarce resources. This is not a textbook in economics.

The word "economic" is a distinct, older term, which English borrowed from the French *économique* and the Latin *economicus*. Originally a noun, but used today only as an adjective, "economic" appears along with a noun that it modifies. Examples include economic forces, economic outcomes, economic relations, and economic events. This book will help you to make sense of economic forces and relations, to grasp the meaning of these events and outcomes as they occur in the world around you. Ultimately the goal of the book is to explain *capitalist economics*, because it turns out that the very nature of "economics" (in the fundamental sense of economic forces and relations) depends on the type of society in which we encounter it. Part I of the book will therefore focus on the question of "economics *in* history," but before starting that work, we first need to familiarize ourselves with this general, older idea of *economicus*.

The basic point is straightforward: economic forces and relations are distinct from other types of relations; they operate according to their own specific mechanisms and rules. One primary aim of this book is to explain and analyze the specific conceptual structure of *economicus* as it operates in capitalist societies, but this means we must understand some simple economic mechanisms and we must make sense out of some straightforward economic forces. Ultimately we will need both to *distinguish* economic forces from other types— physical, social, cultural, or political—and also to show how they are *linked*. But first we will start with a few elementary examples of economic forces or relations. Some of these examples will be expanded upon in great detail in Part II, which devotes entire chapters to them. At that

Capitalist Economics. Samuel A. Chambers, Oxford University Press. © Oxford University Press 2022.
DOI: 10.1093/oso/9780197556887.003.0001

point we will analyze them as *capitalist* economic forces, but here we first get a more general sense of *economicus* by looking at them in the broadest sense.

Money

No one can deny the force of hunger. When your stomach growls, when you have depleted your store of calories, your body's physical need to eat is indisputable. However, *hunger itself is not an economic force*. Regardless of whether we call it biological, physiological, or simply a "natural" force, we need not invoke economic relations in order to make sense out of the human need to eat.

But how do we go about satisfying our hunger? If we happen to find food ready to hand, located in the pantry or the refrigerator, then all we have to do is prepare it and eat. And what if the pantry is bare and the fridge is empty? We could try to grow food in our backyard, but that is impractical at best and impossible at worst; in any case, it would take too long to satisfy our hunger now. Therefore the standard answer is obvious: we go to the store, or to a restaurant, or (if we live in a trendy place) to the nearby food truck.[1] More obvious still, when we get there we will need to present the clerk or the waiter with *money* in order to obtain the food. To satisfy our need for food we must first acquire money; this means that before obtaining our ultimate goal (food), we have an intermediate goal (money).

Your need for money is not natural. You cannot eat money, so there is no way it can directly satisfy your hunger. Money is economic. The fact that you need money in order to overcome hunger explains nothing about you as an individual; it has nothing to do with the nature of your hunger or with the fact that calories from food will satisfy that hunger. Rather, the fact that you need money in order to eat tells you many significant things about the society you live in and the characterization of "food" in that society. It reveals that society as one in which relations to food are mediated by money. Most importantly, **a relation mediated by money is always an economic relation**. Therefore, given the society you live in, satisfying your hunger proves to be economic, not because eating is itself economic but because in the world you inhabit the process of acquiring food to eat depends on obtaining money to buy the food. A society in which food is bought and sold with money is one in which the satisfaction of human hunger can only be carried out through a specific set of economic relations.

We will return to the example of food numerous times throughout this book, and we will explore the nature and importance of money in much more detail, starting with Chapter 4. At this point you should focus on one key takeaway: hunger may be natural, but money is not; the presence or role of money always indicates an economic relation or force.

Price

The economic is not only a type of relation, but also a force that acts on us from outside. We can attempt to alter or thwart this force, but we can never control it directly. We encounter this force (and feel it as external) whenever we buy and sell. If you decide to satisfy your hunger by going to the store to buy bread, peanut butter, and jelly, you will find when you get there that you have no say in the pricing of those items; the prices of all three are written on labels affixed to the items and the shelves. Your choices appear to be confined to the following: pay the price, pick another item to buy, or go home hungry.

There is of course one other very significant option: *steal the food.* This alternative is usually ruled out in our heads—and is therefore excluded from the choices listed in the previous paragraph—because there are laws against theft, laws that establish and protect rights of property. We often think of these laws as separate from economic forces and relations, but even this seemingly silly example demonstrates just the opposite: such laws are crucial preconditions for economic relations. Market prices and market transactions are not fixed or given (not forces of nature), but rather contingent and dependent on a social order that establishes, and defends through force, contractual and legal relations.

If we restrict ourselves for heuristic purposes to the analysis of price as an economic force, we see that the price is *given* to us. We have no choice about it. This logic applies to the case of selling just as much as to buying. It does not matter how much you paid for (or how much you love) your PlayStation console and the many games you are selling with it; when it comes time to list it on eBay or craigslist, the price you receive for it is only as high as someone is willing to pay. It may have taken you months of work to grow tomatoes in your backyard, but if you decide to sell them, the price is the price. People living in the US and much of Europe who tried to sell their houses after the Great Recession had to confront this reality directly and in painful terms: the fact that they paid $400,000 for their house in 2006 and then spent $75,000 to update it in 2007 meant nothing whatsoever when they tried to sell it in 2010—it was only worth $250,000.

Prices are determined not by individuals, and not even by groups of individuals acting consciously to set prices; rather, **prices are determined by multiple economic forces that are beyond the control of any individual or group.** We can call these "market forces" or the "laws" of supply and demand; all that matters at this point is that we see those forces as external, as powerful, and as beyond the realm of direct human choice. Prices are economic.

Profit

Questions about profit—where it comes from, how it is generated, how it is distributed—are the most important economic questions within a capitalist society. You will grapple and engage with these questions in depth in Chapter 6. For now, the point is to see that even when looking at the simplest cases of economic relations in everyday life, the question of profit is never far away.

In our first example, we described how money became our first goal, because we required money before we could satisfy other specific needs or wants. This applies not just to food but to almost everything. Shelter, transportation, clothing, and entertainment can be obtained almost exclusively with money. This means that if we live in a society structured by money, most of our relations will also be economic relations because they will be interwoven with the driving concern of how we get access to money. Fundamental questions about how we live our life, from our career to our various pursuits of happiness, can be traced back to this first question: How do we acquire consistent *streams* of money? We emphasize "streams" because "getting money" is not a one-time act: the money we get today will be spent tomorrow or the next day, and therefore we will soon find ourselves once again needing to get more money. How do we do this?

There are basically two options: get a job or inherit a fortune. If we get a job, then an employer pays us wages. If we inherit a fortune, then we have all the money we need. What does any of this have to do with profit?

Perhaps surprisingly, in both cases our continued flows of money turn out to depend fundamentally on profit. In the case of working a job for a wage, we need the company we work for to remain profitable. If our company stops making a profit, then it may decide to lay us off; worse still (but with the same effect), it may go out of business. In either case, we will no longer receive the stream of money that we depend on in order to live.

And even if we inherit money, we still cannot ignore profit. This is because no one truly "lives off their inheritance" in the sense of directly spending down the money in their inheritance account. No, anyone who inherits or saves up a sum of money will always want to allocate the money in investments that protect the principal balance while adding to it a flow of interest, dividends, and principal growth. But this means that the person who does not work for a wage is even more concerned about profit: they need the businesses they invest in (stocks) or the companies they loan money to (bonds) to continue to earn a profit, because their flow of money depends entirely on those companies' profits.

Whether we work for a wage at McDonald's or on Wall Street, whether we inherit $100 million or borrow a much smaller sum of money to start a business, in every case our future streams of money (and all that they make possible) will be powerfully dependent on the possibility of profit. At its core, profit is the idea that we start with a certain sum of money and turn it into a larger sum of money. **Profit is an important economic phenomenon, and within capitalist societies it is the *essential* economic phenomenon.** You will learn in this book how profit comes about, and you will discover that, like a complex chemical reaction, profit is only possible under very precise conditions and with highly specified variables. For now we emphasize the following root point: no matter where you find yourself in society, profit will matter to you because it will directly affect your ability to acquire the sums of money that you need to live.

Economics Is Not Natural

This book will continually emphasize and illustrate the following central point: economic forces and relations do not, and cannot, exist separately or independently of other forces and relations in society. This means we cannot build up a study of *economicus* as if we were in a laboratory, sealed off from the outside world. Perhaps the study of mathematics and chemistry can begin with elemental particles (numbers and elements). But the elemental particles of economic forces and relations do not exist in nature or in a vacuum; they only exist in a concrete society. Economic relations are not natural relations: they are historical relations that can never be excised or isolated from social, political, cultural, and many other relations.

In searching for their own elemental particle—something to rival chemical elements, or the biological cell—economics textbooks typically begin with some combination of three main notions: *economic goods* (commodities), *scarcity*, and *choice*. The standard story then goes like this: the world is naturally populated with scarce commodities, and economics is the scientific study of how those commodities are allocated efficiently through individual choice.

To repeat: this is not a textbook in economics. Nor is it a point-by-point internal critique of the discipline of economics, which is not to say that it is not *critical* of mainstream economics, but that the main point of this book is to help you understand the world (not to tell you what's wrong with an academic field of study). For these reasons, our exploration of and engagement with *economicus* will mostly ignore the tenets of twenty-first-century economics, either in textbook cases or more sophisticated forms. However, in order to clarify the nature of the journey you will take in the course of this book, it is worth briefly specifying the problems with such attempts to place economics on the foundation of natural or universal "elemental particles." This will help us to distinguish a universal study of "economics" from our grounded engagement with *economicus* as it appears in today's societies—that is, a study of *capitalist economics.*

1. *Commodities (economic goods) are not natural.*

   The earth we inhabit is filled with natural resources: air, water, land, food (from plants and animals), materials for shelter, and numerous energy sources. But natural resources are not immediately economic goods (commodities). In order to become a commodity, a natural resource must enter into economic relations: the material of nature must be transformed (in various ways) in order to *produce* a commodity. **Commodities are not found in nature** in the same way that chemical elements or biological cells are presumed to be.[2] We will explore production in Chapter 2 and later analyze the nature of commodities in great detail, especially in Chapter 5.

2. *Scarcity is an economic relation, not a natural condition.*

   Scarcity is a relative, not an absolute term. To say a resource is "scarce" means that there is not enough of it, given how much is currently needed or desired. This implies a crucial distinction between "limited" and "scarce" resources. Sometimes a limited resource may not be scarce: for example, coal prior to the eighteenth century; pizza, if you order two larges and only you and your roommate show up to eat it. The textbooks that make scarcity the defining starting point of the science of economics are saying not just that resources are finite (that the supply is limited), but that there are *not enough* resources relative to needs/wants. However, **while resources are *limited in nature*, they are only *scarce (or not) within society.*** In other words, scarcity is a real condition, but it is an economic condition—one that can only be understood in terms of economic relations and forces—not a natural condition that would provide the foundation for economics. Scarcity is not a universal starting point.

3. *"Efficiency" is a non sequitur.*

   Standard textbooks often assert that economics seeks the most "efficient" allocation of scarce resources. Yet a system can only be judged as efficient or not relative to a set of predefined ends or goals. Economics long ago borrowed the term *efficiency* from the discipline of physics, wherein efficiency is a simple formula: energy output/energy input. For example, we can easily compare the efficiency of two light bulbs: whichever one has the highest ratio of output (light) relative to input (electricity)—easily measured in lumens per watt—is the most efficient. In economics, the general idea of "efficiency" is that we could compare two different "economies" on the basis of which one produced the most output (commodities) relative to its inputs (natural resources, technical capacities, labor-hours, etc.). And more than this, the economics textbooks claim that economics is the science of maximizing this type of efficiency. But there are at least two huge problems with this approach, both of which you will learn about in detail in this book. First, it is not at all clear how "maximizing economic output" would be a good goal for a society to pursue; do we really want to produce "as many shoes as possible" regardless of the number of people in the country? Second, any measure of efficiency requires consistent, standardized measures of input and output, but economic output is often quantified in terms of *money*, which is not a fixed standard (5 watts is always 5 watts, but $5 can buy more or less at various times). Finally, even if we could solve these problems, we would have to deal with the fact that there is nothing inherent to economic relations or economic forces that necessarily leads to maximizing output or minimizing input. Quite to the contrary, as you will see, not all economic forces and relations are the same: economic forces under feudalism were radically different than those under capitalism. And under capitalism **the inherent trajectory of capitalist economic forces is to** *maximize profits*, **not "efficiency."** Moreover, there is absolutely no reason to believe that more profit creates more efficiency. Overall, given the difficulty of even defining what an "efficient" economic system would be, it turns out that the standard texts are not really saying anything when they say the word "efficiency."

4. *Choice is not uniquely economic.*
    Some textbooks simplify the definition of economics by skipping the idea of scarce commodities and just saying "economics

is the science of choice." Clearly economic relations are dependent on, and in turn help to constrain or enable, various choices made by individuals or groups. If large numbers of Apple customers who previously upgraded their iPhones yearly start choosing to delay their upgrade cycle, it will obviously decrease the overall demand for iPhones. This will lower Apple's sales numbers, which will in turn lower Apple's own purchases from its suppliers, which will then lead Apple to cut back on factory output. If those suppliers then choose to lay off workers, this could impact tens of thousands of workers across the world. If owners of Apple stock choose to sell, this will lower the stock price, which will have an effect not only on the millions of people and organizations that own Apple stock but also on the stock market itself (since Apple makes up roughly 10 percent of the NASDAQ composite index). Choice is surely important to understanding economic forces and relations. However, choices occur everywhere—in politics, in nature, in culture, in families, in society in general—and choices are made according to complex and variegated reasons or logics. **Economics has no monopoly on understanding choice, and not all choices are made according to narrow economic reasoning.** It would be wrong (and a bit hubristic) to presume that all choices were economic choices, and it would be arrogant to think that there could be a "science" that would explain all choices in all domains. To study *economicus* as we will do in this book means to consider a wide range of choices, made according to distinct and changing metrics, and it also means to consider outcomes and distributions that are beyond "choice." Not all economic results can be grasped as the product of individual choice.

"The Economy" Does Not Exist

In rejecting the economics textbooks' efforts to ground a separate science on elemental particles we are simultaneously affirming the fact that economic forces and relations are *always* bound up with, intertwined with, inextricably connected to other sets of relations.

We can look at this point from a different perspective: there is no distinct domain or isolated location in which economic activity takes place. Access any newsfeed and you will see constant references to "the economy," along with apparently limitless data meant to describe the relative health of "the economy." In truth, however, there is no such thing as "the economy." Economic activity occurs not within an "economic domain" but only within society, which means it operates directly alongside and in interaction with other forms of societal activity.

This fact has two important implications. First, we can only study economics within a particular society or set of societies. Economic forces in ancient India looked utterly different from economic forces in medieval Italy, which themselves look almost nothing like economic forces in nineteenth-century Britain. Second, we can say in broader terms that economic forces differ from physical forces: gravity operates the same way in all times and places (although its effects may be very different), but economic relations can only be understood or explained fully for a specific time and place.

Studying Economics as *Economicus*—Overview of the Book

This second point leads to an important conclusion of this introductory chapter. This chapter has tried to familiarize you with a much broader concept of "economics" than one usually finds in textbooks within the discipline of economics. The aim is to explain how economic relations, processes, and forces operate, and to suggest ways to analyze economic events or outcomes. In this introductory chapter we have consciously chosen to use the term *economicus* in order to underscore our sense of economics as constituted by an historically specific set of relations. For the remainder of the book, aside from a few uses to remind us, we will refer simply to "economics" rather than *economicus*, but our understanding of economics will always be informed by these arguments.

This means that for us there simply is no general science of economics because there are no universal (in the sense of transhistorical) economic laws. Furthermore, to study economics as *economicus* means to study it in a particular society or set of societies, at a specific moment in history. In this book then, we will not be studying economics as a general or universal science. Nor will we study *economicus* during the Roman Empire, or in Tang dynasty China. We will be studying economic forces and relations as they have come to exist in modern capitalist societies. As its title makes clear, this book is about *capitalist economics*.

The book is organized and structured so as to build your understanding and knowledge of economic forces, relations, processes, and results. The ultimate goal is to provide you with the tools to understand how economics functions in the society you live in, which means that by the end you should be able to look at everyday practices and events and discern the economic relations that run through and help to explain them.

This leads us to a multipronged approach. First, in Part I we will analyze some of the historical developments that brought about the particular type of economic relations and forces that exist in and across modern capitalist societies today. In other words, we will start with a broader theoretical framework that situates economics within the context of other forces in society as a whole. This conceptual apparatus will be complemented by a brief historical overview that gives the reader a sense of the dramatically different and divergent ways that economic forces have manifested in history. The economic relations that we understand intuitively today, and that we often take for granted, are not universal; those relations only came into existence through a relatively recent process of historical transformation. Put differently, economic forces that we might assume to be natural turn out to be the result of history, and they remain contingent on other social and political relations that were instituted at specific times and places in history.

Next, Part II zooms in on those economic relations in great detail so as to grasp their conceptual nature—to analyze the relations they establish with each other and through which they operate. Each chapter in this section pivots on detailed analysis of one of the key components of *economicus* today: money, commodities, and profit. Part I develops a sense of how economic forces come to operate in the world, and Part II builds on this ground by studying the conceptual structure of the primary elements of capitalism. The aim is to work out a more sophisticated analysis of those economic forces and relations from Part I. Indeed, the ultimate goal of Part II will be to grasp the structure and mechanisms of the most important economic forces operative in the world today: the exchange of commodities, the nature of money, and the key elements of capitalist profit.

Finally, Part III pans out to understand those economic relations in their dynamic interplay with social, cultural, and especially political relations and forces. A rigorous understanding of the fundamental actors within capitalism will make possible a much deeper account of capitalist processes and their broader effects on (and within) a capitalist social order. We will consider the specific mechanisms by which a capitalist society decides to produce a certain set of commodities. This will, in turn, give us some sense of how economic growth or decline occurs for a society as a whole. Part III also strives to offer a clearer sense of some contemporary economic phenomena that often seem bewildering to many people (and which are rarely even addressed in economics textbooks)—particularly financial assets and instruments.

One final note before you dive into the text: unlike some introductory books in the natural and social sciences, where it is possible to skip around from chapter to chapter, this book is not meant to be read out of order. So even if you are most interested in money (Chapter 4) or entrepreneurship (Chapter 7), you will want to start with a careful study of Part I. The commodity (Chapter 5) can only be grasped as a result of the historical development and first emergence of a capitalist system of production; the choices and actions of bankers and central bankers (Chapter 8) can only be explained and unraveled after you have studied money and commodities in Part II. Everything starts with the idea of economics in historical context, so we begin there.

Notes

1. Here and throughout, the "we" refers to the twenty-first-century human beings reading this book, living in modern societies. This "we" is not a generic or universal we that refers to all human beings throughout history. What "we" do to satisfy our hunger is something utterly different than what most humans have done throughout history.

2. Arguably even the most elemental particles of natural science must themselves be understood as imbricated with other types of forces. This issue lies
far beyond the scope of this book, but it raises an important point of emphasis: in rejecting the idea that the economic is "natural," we are not by
any means claiming that it is somehow *unnatural* or separate from material or physical realities. Indeed, as we will see most clearly in Chapter 2,
relations of production and distribution can only be grasped as material,
physical relations, and they are thus utterly bound up with nature—and in
that sense thoroughly "natural." But in the history of economic thought, the
idea of a "natural force" has often been used to distinguish forces and relations within a social order from those that putatively lie beyond it—forces
that are thought somehow to completely and necessarily determine all societal outcomes. It is this final idea that we will reject thoroughly and resist
consistently.

PART I

ECONOMICS *IN* HISTORY

Before we can understand capitalist economics or any other sort of economics, we must first locate economic forces and relations *within history*. Put differently, and in somewhat stronger language, economic forces only come about and always remain conditioned by (dependent on) prior historical change, by earlier social and political transformations. This means that economic forces do not grow, unfold, or "develop" on their own—or according to an independent logic. Rather, as we will explore in this first part of the book, our main "site" for the study of economic forces and relations is society itself.

"Society," however, turns out to be a broad term—sometimes vague and sometimes ambiguous—so in this section of the book we will develop the concept of a "social order." In Chapter 1 we will see that social orders are made up of a variety of forces, relations, and logics: political, social, cultural, and economic. Most significantly, none of these forces are discrete or isolable: each of them functions through, with, and against the others. Economic forces never exist by themselves and can therefore never be fully understood except when grasped in relation to those other forces. Economic forces depend on social and political forces (etc.), and in turn, economic forces will help to reshape or remake cultural and legal relations (etc.).

These changes all occur within history, so when we refer to historical change or "historical development" we are pointing concretely toward these historical transformations. This means that economic relations, including general economic tendencies or "laws," are always contingent upon the political, the cultural, the social, and so on. Changes in economic forces may lead to social and political changes. But the reverse is also true: changes in social, political, and legal relations may create *new* economic forces and relations. For example, political revolution can directly and radically alter the very terms of economics—for example, a democratic revolution that outlaws titles of nobility can utterly undo (literally erase) a key economic category.

Bringing into clear view the concept of a social order located within history will help us to focus our study of economic forces and relations, starting in Chapter 2. There we will demonstrate the following: given that economic forces are part of a larger social order, the most important dimension of economics proves to be not "exchange" but "production." Looking across broad swaths of history, we can see that the first thing that *distinguishes* one economic order from another is not the existence of *markets* for trading goods (we find those almost everywhere in history) but rather the nature and type of *system of production* of goods and services. Exchange remains crucially important, but it must always be understood *in relation to production*.

Chapter 2 will make the case for the "primacy of production" to any understanding of economics, and it will do so by providing a clearer sense of how societies can be radically different from one another because they have distinct "modes of production." As our first opportunity to analyze market exchange in detail—to break it down into its essential components—this chapter will provide one of the central lessons of the entire book: markets can be used for different purposes and therefore the mere existence of markets does not tell us much about the nature of a society. In particular, the presence of markets will not distinguish capitalist societies from noncapitalist ones. But if capitalism is not "free markets" then how do we determine the existence of "capitalism" in the first place?

Part I culminates in Chapter 3, which responds to this fundamental question of capitalism by first answering a prior set of questions: *Where and how does a capitalist social order first emerge historically?* The answer depends on analyzing and making sense of the complex relationship between global markets for exchange, on the one hand, and societal systems of production, on the other. We will see that growth in a particular use of markets (a capitalist use) led to the possibility (but not the inevitability) of a transformation of production. Only that latter transformation, which occurs in England in the sixteenth century, gives us the first appearance of a capitalist social order.

With this original coming into being of capitalism, we can see for the first time what a capitalist social order looks like, which finally gives us the ability to define capitalism. It also sets up everything else that happens in the book. Only against this historical background of the appearance of capitalism *as a unique social order* can we then turn in Parts II and III to a more fine-grained analysis of the structures, principles, and general "rules" of capitalism. That is, the subject of this book, the study of capitalist economics, applies only to capitalist social orders. Part I therefore serves as our foundation.

1

Social Orders and Economic Relations

Robinsonades

Where should we begin a study of *economicus*—what is our starting point for understanding economic forces and relations? Math starts with numbers, biology with cells, literature with stories, but what could serve as the ground for our investigation of economics?

We might seek clues for how to proceed by turning to the modern history of economic thought, which can be roughly divided into two periods:

- Classical Political Economy, running from the seventeenth century to the late nineteenth century.
- Neoclassical Economics, which traces its origins to a major transformation in economic thought—the so-called marginalist revolution of the 1870s—and runs all the way to the present day.

Despite the significant differences between these two paradigms, they offer strikingly similar responses to our primary question here—namely, where to start. Let's look quickly at two quotations from writings in the history of economic thought:

1. "This division of labour . . . is not originally the effect of any human wisdom. . . . It is the necessary, though very slow and gradual, consequence of a certain propensity in human nature, which has in view no such extensive utility; **the propensity to truck, barter, and exchange** one thing for another."
2. "Economists normally assume that people are rational. Rational people systematically and purposefully do the best they can to

Capitalist Economics. Samuel A. Chambers, Oxford University Press. © Oxford University Press 2022.
DOI: 10.1093/oso/9780197556887.003.0002

achieve their objectives, given the available opportunities. . . . A **rational decision maker takes an action if and only if the marginal benefit of the action exceeds the marginal cost.**"

Aside from the clue provided by use of the now-archaic word "truck" (a synonym for barter and exchange), it might be hard to tell that these quotations are separated by 240 years. The first is the opening lines from the second chapter of *The Wealth of Nations* (1776), Adam Smith's canonical text in classical political economy; the second is the third of ten principles of economics in the first chapter of Gregory Mankiw's *Principles of Microeconomics* (2016) textbook. A clear and central focus on human individual actors and their fundamental, systematic characteristics unites these disparate texts across almost a quarter millennium of history. Put simply, both texts start with the inherent nature of the individual and build an abstract account of economics from that foundation. Here is their logic: *given* that the individual has a natural inclination to barter and exchange, economic relations can be logically *derived* directly from the individual. In general, economic forces are natural; in particular, economics has its foundation in human nature. Overall, economic forces can be understood as emerging from the natural actions, choices, and inclinations of (rational) human beings. This approach serves to link the study of economics to the study of modern politics: both ground their projects on the concept of a "state of nature," a place outside of time and history where we can observe the true, *natural* tendencies of humans. In politics, state-of-nature theorists tell us that humans are naturally free and equal; in economics, state-of-nature theorists tell us that human beings naturally exchange, maximize benefits, and "think at the margin."

There's just one problem with this story. It's based on fiction, on fairytale, on myth; it's utterly made up. To be clear, the mistake is not merely that the story is false, that there never was such a time in which humans lived in such a state. The mistake is that the story of a state of nature posits an isolated and ahistorical human being with supposedly natural characteristics, when such an individual, to the limited extent that he or she exists, actually only comes to be at a very particular time and place within a very peculiar type of society.

In fact, the story of a "state of nature" that has been repeated throughout the history of economic thought proves to be merely a variation on a much broader literary genre—the Robinsonade. "Robinsonade" is the name given to the genre of literary tale that began in the seventeenth century and flourished after the publication of Daniel Defoe's famous novel *Robinson Crusoe* (1719). It is a shipwreck or castaway story (or in later forms, a space story) in which the protagonist suddenly finds himself removed from society and forced to survive in "nature."

To ground an account of economics on the propensities of individuals as located in a state of nature means to use the terms of the Robinsonade genre as the foundation of a universal economic theory. Despite intentions, this move establishes the theory not on the universal characteristics of human beings but in the very specific and very peculiar characteristics of the protagonist in a literary genre. This seems a strange and weak starting point for the theory, and it presumes exactly what we ought to try to explain (humans exchanging resources that they find in nature). We should remember that there were no such stories prior to the seventeenth century. If humans are universally exchanging and cost–benefit maximizing creatures, then why did no one prior to this (rather late) point in history recognize such a supposedly transhistorical fact? The earliest candidate for establishing the Robinsonade genre was a work published in England in the middle of the seventeenth century, so perhaps we should ask ourselves what happened around that place and time in history. One important answer: capitalism appeared for the first time. We will return to this crucial point in Chapter 3.

Social Orders

For now, if we want to understand capitalist economics we have to begin from a completely different place than the Robinsonade. **Human beings have never lived in a "state of nature." They have only ever lived in societies.** As we look back across the wide expanse of human history, we never find isolated, individual human beings. We only find groups of humans, *living together* in some form of social order and at varying degrees of scale: from tribes, to villages, to cities, to nations, to empires.

The "nature" of any individual human can only be grasped within the context of the social order in which we locate them. In some historical forms of social order we can certainly find individuals who trade goods, almost always by buying and selling them with money. But in most examples of social orders across history we find individuals much more likely to give goods to one another, or simply to produce them directly for the larger social unit (e.g., the tribe). Whatever we ultimately want to say about specific types of economic relations and forces, we first have to *locate* them within a concrete social order.

Because economic relations are socially and historically contingent, this book centers on *capitalist* economic relations: it focuses on the relations that arise when a social order is structured and arranged in the unique pattern and form of a capitalist society. We will repeatedly observe that a capitalist social order is structured differently, and therefore *generates different economic forces*, than other forms of social order. And we will be able to sharpen our view of the precise workings of capitalist economics by comparing and contrasting them with the economics of distinct social orders.

All of this leads to a direct answer to our opening question. In our effort to understand economic relations and forces, we must start in the only place we can start: the "social order" in which those relations emerge.

Grounding Economic Relations in History

At first glance, our starting point looks less solid than the one suggested by Smith and Mankiw. By beginning with the autonomous individual thought to be endowed with universal characteristics (the propensity to exchange, the rationality to calculate costs and benefits), they are able to set history aside completely. Nonetheless, as we saw, their solid ground proved shaky when we noticed a literary myth underlying it. The specifically historical nature of the literary genre of the Robinsonade belies the purportedly universal claims of the textbooks.

In contrast, we must always remain attentive to historical context and historical developments. By grounding economic relations in social orders, we are also *situating* economics within historical context. Our starting point in social orders leads us to insist that **there are no universal, ahistorical economic forces.** Because economic forces operate within concrete social orders, any relations, tendencies, or "laws" of economics will themselves be *contingent.* To describe those relations as contingent does not make them invalid; it merely marks out the terrain and temporality of their validity.[1] As we will see, certain feudal economic forces simply will not operate in capitalist social orders, and in turn, the capitalist economic relations that we will study in this book remain valid only within capitalist social orders. Feudal and capitalist social orders are characterized by different *types* and *arrangements* of economic forces. As such, the economic relations that we will study in this book are specific to a social order that is itself capitalist.

We must emphasize, however, that historical contingency proves to be a unique strength of our approach, and not at all a weakness. In addition to grounding our account of economic relations and forces within history, we also make it possible **to explain economic historical development.** Thus, in the coming chapters, we will be able to answer a question that Smith and Mankiw never even try to ask themselves: Why did people start writing Robinsonades in the seventeenth century? What changes were occurring in the particular social order that would lead fiction authors to imagine the very idea of a Robinson Crusoe (a thoroughly civilized subject of the British Empire) stranded on an island?

How Do We Explain Economic Relations?

The question of starting point remains linked to a broader and more significant methodological question: *How do we explain?* Traditional approaches to teaching economics rest on a method of **linear, causal** explanation. The method starts with an independent variable, where "independent" indicates the unique primacy of this variable—it requires no prior explanation itself (it is given). This model of explanation draws a line (hence "linear") from the independent variable to a dependent variable: $A \to B$. At the core of the explanation lies the claim that A *causes* B, which usually means not that the existence of A causes B to exist, but rather that some *change* in A causes a *change* in B. Changes in B are therefore *dependent* upon changes in A (which is itself *independent*). If B changes in the same direction—that is, it goes up when A goes up—then we can call the relation *positive*, and if B moves in the opposite direction we call the relation *negative*. Importantly, the change in A must be considered "exogenous," meaning that such a change lies outside the realm of explanation.[2] Causal linear explanation provides the core for much work in economics and across the social sciences; indeed, it proves so ubiquitous that most of us treat it as intuitively obvious.

Let's look at two examples of this type of explanation. The first proves very general; the second is a specific variation on the first—one that has proved central to mainstream economics, and that we will later (in Part II) rethink significantly.

1. An increase in the supply of a good leads to a decrease in its price.

   Supply is the independent variable: we won't ask how or why it changes, but take it as a given. Price is the dependent variable: its change is caused by the change in supply. We can easily write this out in a formal language that describes the economic relation while expressing the causal linear model of explanation.

   $G \uparrow \to P_g \downarrow$ [G = quantity of good; P_g = price of good]

2. An increase in the money supply leads to a decrease in the price of money.

   $M \uparrow \to P_m \downarrow$ [M = quantity of money; P_m = price of money]

   At first glance this appears to be the exact same relation as in point 1, and the core of the explanation is in fact identical. The discipline of economics takes money to be a good like any other,[3] so an increase in its supply leads to a decrease in its price. However, money is a unique "good," and the "price of money" is a unique price. Money proves unique because the price of all other goods is measured in terms of money, so if the price or value of money drops (if money is worth less than it was before), the price of all other goods goes up. If a cup of coffee costs $2 today, and overnight the "price of money" or the value of money goes down by 50 percent, then tomorrow we will need more money to acquire a cup of coffee (assuming its price/value has not changed). This means that tomorrow it will take $3 to buy a cup of coffee. The price of coffee has gone up because the "price of money" went down. But it's not just coffee: since *every* good's price depends on money, a decrease in money's value leads to an increase in the price of all goods; the cost of everything increases. We can therefore say that with an increase in M (money supply) the overall price level, P, goes up. And an increase in the price level (the prices of all goods) is the very definition of **inflation**. So we can rewrite our formula above, substituting P (price level) for P_m (the price of money): $M \uparrow \to P \uparrow$ Or, in ordinary language: an increase in the supply of money leads to inflation.

Both of these linear, causal explanations have played a central role in the history of economic thought. The first point describes the core idea of the basic "laws" of supply and demand. The second point describes the "quantity theorem of money"—the most widely distributed and influential (on policy choices) conceptual account of money in history.

Which Comes First: Social Orders or Economic Relations?

Almost everyone can identify the Achilles' heel of linear causal explanation. It is the problematic question "which comes first," and we see it in everyday discourse expressed in terms of "the chicken and the egg problem" or the mantra that "correlation is not causation." The basic point is simple: we frequently observe simultaneous changes in two distinct phenomena. But the linear causal model of explanation only explains anything if we can (a) isolate one phenomenon, (b) show that its changes are primary and independent (thus making it the independent variable), and (c) articulate the causal mechanism by which this independent variable directly causes changes in the dependent variable.

To explain economic forces and relations, and to understand economic changes as they occur in history, our overarching approach in this book will be different from standard social science methods. We will not start with abstract and general principles and then build models based on those principles. Instead, let's start here with some specific commentary on these two examples of linear causal explanation.

1. $G \uparrow \rightarrow P_g \downarrow$

It is absolutely true that *most of the time* (not always) when the quantity of a good available for purchase increases, its price will tend to go down. But it is important to be clear that this relationship between quantity and price is not an intrinsic property of the good itself. For example, there is nothing within the chemical structure or other physical properties of a loaf of bread to indicate that either (a) there are more loaves of bread available or (b) its price must be lower. The price depends on human actions (what individuals and groups do), which itself depends on a broader social context (what's going on). The price of goods *tends* to go down with increases in supply because the sellers of the goods find that potential buyers were already buying as much bread as they wanted; in order to induce those buyers to buy more (or nonbuyers to become buyers), the sellers must compete with one another by lowering the price. So the change does not come about intrinsically; it depends entirely on the changes in relations between sellers and buyers. Here then we provide a deeper explanation of the relationship established by the causal/linear model.

Perhaps more significantly, however, we cannot always (and simply) begin with a change in quantity. We have to ask: Why did the producers of bread (the large bread manufacturers, the artisan bakers, etc.) bake more bread? Changes in the quantity of goods do not happen randomly. Contrary to the assumptions of the linear/causal model, changes in quantity are never really exogenous. They do not come from "outside" the system of economic forces and relations; quite the opposite, those changes are themselves spurred or provoked within the system. If the quantity of loaves of bread increases, then to understand the economic phenomenon we need to find out why. Did the number of producers stay the same while each increased output? Did most producers keep output constant while a small number of producers increased output dramatically? Did the producers from the previous period of production bake the same amount of bread while a number of new producers entered the market? (Good answers to these questions will require analysis of social, cultural, and political forces—not just economic forces.)

Crucially, the answer to these questions will not end our explanation simply by providing one more link in a linear causal chain (e.g., output of producers goes up, so we have $O \uparrow \rightarrow G \uparrow \rightarrow P_g \downarrow$). Once we have discovered that current producers increased their output, we then want to know why. Did they anticipate greater overall demand for bread? If so, why? And why were they wrong about that expectation?[4] Here we notice something essential: the basic causal relation, $G \uparrow \rightarrow P_g \downarrow$, will not hold at all if demand increases at the same time, since the increase in demand will offset the increase in supply, thus keeping prices the same or even increasing them. And once we start asking about *why* supply increases, we see that one of the primary reasons will be **an anticipation by producers of increased demand**; hence it may turn out to be the case that more often than not an increase in the supply of goods does not lead to a decrease in price.

The point is not to *disprove* this relationship but to undermine the idea that it is a simple linear/causal relation. Any relationship between supply and price only ever exists within a complex social order, embedded in a larger historical context: the decisions that producers of goods and purchasers of goods make depend upon that context. Rather than try to build up an economic model of explanation from these fundamental linear/causal relations, our approach to explaining economic forces and relations insists that **there are no fundamental linear/causal relationships**. There are only complex and multicausal relations. This means that price is not simply determined by quantity, it is multiply determined—or better, *overdetermined*—by a host of factors. To say that an outcome, such as the change in price, is "overdetermined" means that there are so many different factors that could lead to its change that we *can never predict* a change in the future. All we can ever do is to explain the change after it has occurred, by tracing it in complex ways to a variety of factors that helped bring it about.

2. $M \uparrow \rightarrow P \uparrow$

As described previously, this formula describes the "quantity theorem of money." We can unpack this theorem as follows:

   a. Money is a commodity like any other commodity, subject to the same basic laws of supply and demand.

   b. An increase in the supply of money leads to a decrease in its price.

   c. A decrease in the price of money is just another name for inflation, since both express the idea that the costs of all commodities (except for money) are increasing.

   d. Any increase in the supply of money (whether it be the discovery of gold or the "printing of money" by a central bank) will lead to inflation.

The linear/causal model of explanation makes this theorem appear true almost by definition: if money is a commodity, an increase in its supply must cause inflation. Because it seems inarguable, numerous economists throughout history have defended the quantity theorem. But we know the theorem will not hold. It has been empirically disproven. From 2009 to 2014 the money supply in the United States increased fourfold, but inflation remained extremely low.[5] This false causal relation can serve as a helpful example for us. It can illuminate both the general weaknesses of the linear/causal model of explanation and the specific problems with this explanation of money and inflation.

In the following chapters we will explore the following points:

1. Money is not a commodity and cannot be treated as such. Money is a radically different kind of entity (utterly unlike a commodity), and, even under strict so-called ceteris paribus conditions, money is not subject to the "laws" of supply and demand.

2. To the extent that we can track a relation between the overall amount of money and overall price levels, we see that the quantity theorem of money has the relationship backwards: it is not the quantity of money that causes a change in price levels, but rather a change in the price levels that causes a change in the quantity of money.

3. This is why, as advocates of the quantity theorem of money have pointed out, it is true that when we look at historical examples of inflation (particularly hyperinflation), we see a massive increase in the quantity of money.

4. Changes in the price level lead to changes in the quantity of money, and changes in the price level can and must therefore be explained quite separately from the variable of "money supply."

Despite the subtleties and complexities of the example of money and inflation (which we will return to in Parts II and III), as our takeaways here we can focus on the basic question of how to explain economic phenomena. There can be no adequate explanation of economic forces and relations that does not situate itself within the context of a particular social order; this requires connecting any changes in economic relations to the overall system of production within that social order. If prices drop, we cannot simply assume that supply increased exogenously; we have to understand the particular changes in supply, track those to the decisions and planning of producers, and link those back in turn to the choices and actions of purchasers and potential purchasers of goods and services.

We can see here that economic relations are more often than not circular; they are never linear.[6] Producers do not act independently of the actions of buyers. Quite the opposite: producers make long-term plans for what, how, and how much to produce based explicitly on both the past actions of buyers and, crucially, the producers' projections, forecasts, and anticipations of buyers' future actions. Therefore, to continue to develop our own model of economic explanation, and to expand our account of social orders as the context for economic forces and relations, Chapter 2 focuses on the question of how a social order *produces*.

Notes

1. Even the laws of physics turn out to be "contingent" in an important sense: given the differences in atmosphere and gravitational force, physical relations and patterns valid on one planet will not be valid on another. In an analogous way, the transition from one economic order to another is, as far as economic forces and relations are concerned, like moving to another planet. Physics, of course, also tries to identify laws that are valid across the entire universe. Our point here is that there are no such universal laws that would describe economic forces and relations.

2. When expressing a linear, causal relation between two variables, economists often include the Latin phrase ceteris paribus, which literally means "other things equal." Within the terms of the model of linear, causal explanation, the phrase is better understood as "all other variables held constant." In other words, the ceteris paribus conditions posit that a relationship between the two variables can be isolated from all other variables, from all other elements of social and political order, and from all other aspects of historical change. We can say that a specific change in *A causes* a specific change in *B* if and only if we also assume that there are no other variables influencing either *A* or *B*.

3. In Chapters 4 and 5 we will return to this assumption, disprove it, and explore the implications for how we understand money and commodities.

4. In Chapter 9 we will briefly discuss a crucial supply/demand counter-example, a case where a decrease in demand was followed by an *increase* in price. Importantly, this example is not at all random or minor; it comes from the recent past (2015–2019) and it centers on the Apple iPhone.

5. Strong adherence to the quantity theorem also provides one of the many reasons that so many people were buying bitcoins in 2020 and 2021. Despite the evidence from the Great Recession, some remain convinced that the increase in the "supply" of money must, almost definitionally, lead to inflation. In this context, many felt that the limited supply of bitcoins would make them a hedge against this inflation, or that bitcoins would have stable inherent value because their numbers were limited. Our exploration of the nature of money in Chapter 4 will provide a conceptual argument that challenges the quantity theorem and complements the empirical evidence against it.

6. Within the terms of the linear/causal model, to call an explanation "circular" is to reject and refute it precisely because the rules of the linear/causal model require that we start with an independent variable (which is

not itself *caused*) and then move to the dependent variable (which does not itself *cause*). To suggest that effects end up redounding back on their own causes is to entirely undermine linear/causal explanation. In saying (in the text above) that the relations between production and exchange constantly interact, that each causes and is caused by the other, we take our leave entirely from the linear/causal model. Our task must be to explain economic phenomena differently, to show how we can still understand, make sense of, and grasp economic forces and relations without falling back on an untenable linear/causal model. This will require us to explain and make sense of circular relations, rather than using the term "circular" as a pejorative.

2

How Societies Produce

Economic Activities

We have now *situated* our study of economic forces and relations within the wider context of social orders, within the structures of society. Economic forces and relations are always entangled with social, political, and cultural forces and relations. As discussed in the Introduction, "the economy" is not a thing. There is no domain where economic forces operate separately or on their own; they only ever operate with, through, against, and alongside a variety of other forces. Rather than start with a fictitious "economy," we have to begin with a real society, with concrete social orders.

This means that our method inverts the standard method of modern economics: rather than begin with a simple, isolated individual who operates in a supposedly pure economic realm, and then build up systems and rules from that basis, we must start with a broad and complex social order, and then attempt to bore down into it—to locate the economic forces that operate within and across it. In Chapter 1 we worked at a very high level of abstraction to describe the concept of a social order and to make sense of how we could analyze and explain economic forces within societies. In Part II we will narrow our focus significantly by looking closely at three essential elements/components of *economicus* (money, commodities, and profit). In this chapter we will work in the intermediate space between those two, operating at the "meso level." Our goal is to get a better sense of how to recognize economic forces and to distinguish them (which is not the same thing as separating them or rendering them distinct) from other types of forces.

To achieve this aim we can take a page out of the playbook of classical political economy. The classical political economists generally understood economics to be divisible into a few distinct realms,

Capitalist Economics. Samuel A. Chambers, Oxford University Press. © Oxford University Press 2022.
DOI: 10.1093/oso/9780197556887.003.0003

typically categorized as follows: production, distribution, exchange, and consumption. However, these four categories are easily reduced to two: first, by excluding "consumption" from economics since the consumption of a commodity goes on in "private" (it only occurs *after* the economic [trans]actions have been completed); second, by ignoring distribution as either a minor, technical matter (how goods are transported from their location of production to their site of sale) or a separate moral or political question (a question of why distribution always seems so unequal). This leaves us with production and exchange as the primary economic activities. In classical political economy (again, from the seventeenth through the nineteenth centuries) some authors focused more on production, while others emphasized exchange.

But with the transition to the neoclassical paradigm (toward the end of the nineteenth century), the realm of exchange (of the market) became the primary, central, and often exclusive locus of economics. During the "marginalist revolution" a number of economists attempted to use calculus equations (ones they had illicitly borrowed from abandoned physics models) in an attempt to model a state of "general equilibrium" in exchange, a static "moment." In this moment of equilibrium, supply = demand, price is "given" by the market, and the market (for goods and services) "clears" in the sense that all sellers find buyers (and vice versa) at the market price. Put simply, neoclassical economics attempts to explain all economic forces and relations in terms of this singular model of equilibrium—an approach that makes exchange not just the primary but almost the exclusive domain of economics. With the modern economics of the neoclassical paradigm, economics *is* market exchange.

This is not to say that modern economics never discusses production; the point is, rather, that it explains even production through models based entirely on exchange. Exchange becomes the secret core of all economic forces and relations. Anyone who has taken an introductory economics course has encountered this as the first lesson of most textbooks, as it appears in the "guns and butter" chart (or "production possibility frontier")—often the very first chart in the book. This simple chart presents societal production as itself a consumer choice. Just as a buyer in exchange must choose between spending a given income on clothes versus food, on entertainment versus necessities (on pizza or Coke), so a society—according to this lesson—has to choose how much of its overall resources to devote to the production of "butter" (metaphorically representing social welfare) or "guns" (representing security).

The guns and butter chart offers a simple and straightforward model of societal production, based on the concept of a "production function." Such an approach has the advantage of rendering production and exchange isomorphic—hence all economic actions look just like the actions that a consumer makes in the marketplace. But the main problem with the idea of a production function is that it bears almost no relation to reality whatsoever. The actual concrete activity of production (under capitalism, but also under other social orders) looks nothing like the guns and butter chart. And the reason is simple: producing goods and services is not the same type of activity as buying and selling produced goods and services. Decisions about whether, when, and how to take up the process of producing a good or service cannot be understood or explained using the same logic as one might use to try to explain why a consumer buys one commodity rather than another. You cannot explain production through a model of exchange equilibrium.

In broader terms, we can locate a fundamental reason that it proves impossible to give a *general* account of economic forces and relations that centers on exchange: there is never anything to exchange (to buy or to sell) until after it has been produced. Here we see with more force why Robinsonades are so misleading. In a state-of-nature story, "economic actors" (i.e., human beings, who are naturally exchanging creatures) simply find "economic goods" lying around. One effect of the literary tale is to treat natural resources (apples growing on an apple tree, a deer running in the forest) as if they were nothing other than capitalist commodities. Starting with the myth of the state of nature leads mainstream economics, quite logically, to conclude that all economic activity boils down to exchange. But if we look to the world we live in, or if we turn to examples of concrete societies—located in specific times and places in history—we find that economic goods do not exist in nature: *someone has to make them.*

The Primacy of Production

When focusing on exchange, it's easy to conceive of the basic unit of society (and of economics) as a solitary, autonomous economic actor, often referred to as *homo economicus*—"economic man," a human creature defined by her or his capacity to choose among scarce economic goods.[1] But if we leave the domain of exchange and closely consider the basic problem of production, we cannot escape the immediate conclusion: individual human beings are not self-sufficient; they can never produce on their own. **All production is social production.** Production only comes about within a social order that has some system (however rough or tacit) of organizing production processes.

By insisting that economic forces and relations only exist within society, we make it plain to see that a society's "commodity set" (the total amount of goods and services) does not exist naturally; it must be created, manufactured—produced economically. Moreover, production itself proves complex since to "produce" a commodity does not mean to "choose" it, but rather to initiate a complicated process that requires both time and money. In market exchange the decision to purchase is almost instantaneous with taking possession of the commodity. Here we can think of the "buy it now" button, patented by Amazon in 1999, which nicely expresses the way in which—within the terms of market exchange—"choosing" becomes equivalent to "having." Indeed, if what I'm buying is a Kindle e-book or an Amazon music track, that single click includes not only decision and possession but also consumption, as the book will download to my Kindle and open immediately to the first page.

Time is not an issue (or only a minor issue, as I have to wait for shipping) within the realm of exchange. But in the realm of production we find a completely different story. In production, the decision to begin the process may come weeks, months, years, sometimes even decades before the commodity itself comes into existence and can then be offered for sale on the market. Production is neither instantaneous nor timeless; it has a very specific temporality. Production occurs over a particular period of time—known, simply enough, as a period of production.

Beyond this crucial temporal aspect, the logical structure and concrete practices of production turn out to be very much *distinct* from those of exchange. Most importantly, and contrary to the ambitions of the neoclassical model of "general equilibrium," neither production nor exchange can be explained in terms of the other. Each depends on the other (we exchange what has been produced, and, at least under capitalism, we produce *for* exchange), so they must be understood relationally, but neither can be *reduced* to the other; each must be understood under its own terms as a unique process.

Here, and throughout this book, we seek to demonstrate a further point: production is not merely distinct from exchange, **production is primary**. Not only does production begin the economic cycle, not only does production come first, but also in the overall economic system of production, distribution, exchange, and consumption, **the most important element is production**. This is the case because when we look at the economic forces and relations that operate across a social order, *what matters most, in the sense of distinguishing one economic order from another*, is not how individuals trade, exchange, or buy/ sell goods. Rather, the most important element of an economic order is how, and according to what system and rules and structures, those goods are produced in the first place.[2]

Modes of Production

The "primacy of production" thesis points not merely to the fact that in a given economic timeline production always happens prior to exchange (goods can only be exchanged *after* they have been produced), but, much more significantly, that what distinguishes one socioeconomic order from another is the nature of production. In a general sense, any society has what we can call a *mode of production*. "Mode of production" names the broad structures, systems, techniques, and practices by which the overall societal output gets created. It is the answer to the question, "how does a (particular) society produce?" In the following chapters, this book will commonly refer to the overall "system of production" or to the process of production, both of which are synonyms for "mode of production." All of these ideas help to underscore the primacy of production by highlighting production as the main marker of economic difference across societies; societies may share techniques for distribution, exchange, and consumption, but differ radically in how they produce.

Let's look at an example: a very general comparison between the economic systems of early fifteenth-century France and late nineteenth-century America. How did each of these societies produce? In 1454 France, production was mainly the production of basic necessities (especially food), and the primary agents of that production were *serfs*. Serfs worked the land of *lords*. Serfs were *bonded* to the lords in a relation of unfreedom and servitude, as they were **required by both law and social custom to produce** for their lords. The lords' titles to the land and to its produce were themselves established by law, by political power, and by moral custom. Most significantly, the lords' rights were granted by monarchs (kings and queens) who held sovereign power over all the land. This means that there was no such thing as "private property" as we understand it today. The land was ruled by the king, who delegated rights to the land (but not ownership of it) to lords. In this general "mode of production," serfs produced food and basic necessities directly; they did so not only for themselves and their families but also for their lords and their lords' families. The bulk of production was therefore *internal* to the fiefdoms of lords. Distribution was merely distribution from the serf to the lord, and within the lordly estate there was no exchange. While there were also external trading markets for luxuries and certain other specialty goods, the vast majority of goods were produced for direct consumption, not for the market. We can call this a **feudal mode of production.**

In contrast, in America in 1877, the subject positions of "lord" and "serf" simply did not exist. There were no fiefdoms, no manors, no royal titles, and thus no estates. The social, legal, and political relations that established feudal estates, lordly rights, and serf bondage had all been obliterated. Property was now owned privately, that is individually, and the individual right to property was itself the first principle (property was not a privilege granted by the political sovereign but itself a prior claim against the political sovereign). These legal and property relations radically changed the nature of production. Small farmers could produce for themselves directly, and in the early history of America this was more common. But by 1877, most production was production for exchange. That is, almost all production was production *for the market*; goods were not produced to be consumed by the producer (or his lord) but produced with the primary intention of being sold on the market—and sold at a profit. The key categories in this mode of production were thus totally different from the categories in the feudal mode of production. Rather than lords and serfs, we find at this place and time "workers" and "enterprise owners." Workers were actively and directly involved in production, yet they did not create goods for themselves or for those they were linked to within society. Enterprise owners planned and oversaw the production process but did not produce directly themselves, nor did they have direct political or legal powers over workers. Rather, the law established a certain rough equality between workers and owners.[3] That is, workers were not legally bound (as were serfs) to work for owners but were instead allowed to enter into wage contracts freely as they saw fit.

The fifteenth-century French serf produced goods for himself and his lord; that is, the goods were never exchanged, but instead went directly to consumption by people who lived on the same land. **The nineteenth-century American worker produced goods for strangers**, for people she did not know and would never even meet. The goods produced by this worker could only reach their destination by way of market exchange. Indeed, the goods were directly produced for that market; **they were produced in order to be sold.** The French serf worked the land as a matter of legal obligation, and those social and legal relations also entailed that part of the serf's production went directly to him and his family. The American worker freely contracted to work for an owner and to be paid an hourly wage; the product of her labor was, by contractual definition, immediately owned by the enterprise owner or entrepreneur who paid the worker's wages.

Production within the French feudal system was organized and executed both outside of market exchange and with very little regard for market forces or mechanisms. In contrast, in the American enterprise system almost everything was mediated, constrained, or driven by the market; all production depended on the market, and all production was oriented to the market.

Not All Markets Are Capitalist Markets

This basic example calls our attention to a crucial point: the existence of a "market" to exchange goods tells us very little about a social order's economic system. Markets for the trade of economic goods have existed for thousands and thousands of years, and markets appear in (or, usually, at the edges of) a wide variety of dramatically different social orders and economic systems. This draws us to a powerful, if for many, counterintuitive, conclusion: if we want to locate the specificity of a capitalist social order (to find the elements of that order that make it distinct from others), markets will not do us any good. **Capitalist societies are not at all unique in having markets for the free exchange of goods and services.** Put simply, capitalism cannot be adequately described as a "free market system," because many noncapitalist societies also had free markets.

In the next chapter we will trace the history of the first emergence of a capitalist social order. And in Part II we will analyze in detail the mechanisms, structures, and forces that make up a capitalist social order. For now we only need to cover a more elementary point, which is that *what distinguishes a capitalist society from a noncapitalist one is not the existence of markets but the use and function of markets **and their relation to the mode of production**.* Capitalist societies prove unique not because of how they exchange but because of how they structure and orient production toward the goal of exchange. To think this point through, let us return to the rough example of 1454 France.

In late medieval, feudal France, the aim of the overall system of production had very little to do with markets. The system of production was set up to provide direct sustenance for serfs, and to provide both sustenance, *and a surplus*, for lords. Put differently, since lords did not engage in productive activities directly, the feudal system was built on a system of overt and explicit political and economic domination, in the form of the extraction of surplus product distributed from the serf to the lord. In certain manifestations of feudalism, this fact of surplus extraction was expressed quite clearly in that specific days of the week were set aside for the serf to work the land for his own benefit, with other days specifically designated for him to work the land for the benefit of his lord. Overall, the aim of production under feudalism had little to do with markets. This does not mean markets did not exist, nor that they were not important to society, but it helps us to understand something crucial about the basic function of markets in a noncapitalist society.

In a word, markets in such societies did exactly what economics textbooks tell us markets are supposed to do. They allowed individuals to trade goods: to sell good A (which they had too much of) and buy good B (which they had too little of). Markets therefore allow for a redistribution of economic goods, and this may lead to a more "optimal allocation" of resources across the society because multiple parties may improve their individual positions through market exchange. But it proves crucial to understand fully the nature of this type of market exchange. Let's try to map it out in clear terms.

When we come to a market to trade, to swap one commodity for another, we are looking to trade *equivalents*. If I have lots of oats that I've harvested but would prefer to eat something more than oats for dinner tonight, I could seek out someone with lots of peas. When we agree to trade, I am hoping to get **an equivalent** amount of peas for my oats, while my trading partner is hoping to get **an equivalent** amount of oats for her peas. For me the transaction looks like this: $C_o \rightarrow C_p$. I give the oats commodity for the peas commodity, or as the symbols suggest, I seem to *transform* oats into peas. For her it looks like this: $C_p \rightarrow C_o$. But if we take one step back we can clearly see that neither of these transformations would be possible unless somehow (a particular amount of) oats are equal to (a particular amount of) peas. In symbols: $C_o = C_p$.[4]

If our trade of oats for peas is a fair one, if no one cheats the other, then at the completion of the transaction each of us has received an equal amount of what was given. This means obviously—but as we will see, quite importantly—no one has increased their overall stock of commodities; each of us has merely changed the composition. *No one has gotten more.* And this means it would be impossible to *grow* the total value of our commodities merely through basic market exchange, $C \rightarrow C$. Finally, there are two important amendments to this conclusion about the exchange of equivalents.

First, and more straightforwardly, even if the exchange is not equal, even if one party does get the better of the other on the trade (or if one party cheats outright), this doesn't change the fundamental fact that the **trade itself does not increase total value**. Let's say I have 20 pounds of oats and you have 40 pounds of peas, and that 1 pound of oats is worth twice as much as 1 pound of peas. This means that the total values of each of our "commodity sets" (my oats and your peas) are equal, and it also indicates that a fair trade between us would require you to give me peas for oats at a two-to-one ratio (i.e., you give me 2 pounds of peas for every 1 pound of oats I give you). But let's say you are very smart and trick me into trading you 10 pounds of oats for 10 pounds of peas. The result is that your total commodity set (30 pounds of peas and 10 pounds of oats) has gone up in value (by 25 percent) and my total commodity set (10 pounds of oats and 10 pounds of peas) has gone down in value (by 25 percent). But the cumulative value of our two commodity sets has not changed at all. The unfair trade is zero-sum; my loss is your gain. Total value does not increase (or decrease).

Second, and more portentously, **the introduction of money does not alter the type of market exchange we have been describing here**, but it does make possible a radically different use of the market.[5] In the basic market exchange we have been describing, money is nothing more than a technical invention that facilitates the same basic form of exchange. Here again we repeat what standard economic textbooks all tell us: crude barter of one commodity for another proves highly cumbersome. If I come to the market with only oats but desire to leave it with not only peas but also rice, bread, and socks, then I am forced to haul my oats around the market hoping to find sellers of all of those commodities—sellers who just happen to want oats. It would obviously be more convenient if the first step I made at the market were to find someone who would give me *money* for my oats,[6] which I could then use as a currency to purchase all the other commodities I need and want. Money changes our basic formula as follows: rather than $C \to C$, we will have $C \to M \to C$. Money *mediates* the exchange of basic commodities. The starting point and end point are the same: I began with only oats and finished up with oats and peas, but in between I transformed my oats first into money and then into peas.

This leads us to both a general conclusion about market exchange and a specific conclusion about its relation to production. In broad terms, markets merely facilitate the exchange of equivalent commodities, $C \rightarrow C$. This sort of system of exchange could potentially play some (small or large) part in any economic order, regardless of the mode of production. The existence of exchange markets is not sufficient to tell us anything definitive about the mode of production or to determine the overall socioeconomic order. Thus, we have seen in the specific case of fifteenth-century French feudalism that the primary mode of production did not involve exchange at all. Nevertheless, the feudal mode of production does not preclude the existence of markets for exchange, particularly of luxury or rare goods. Here we clarify and sharpen our earlier point about the primacy of production: in comparing and contrasting 1454 France with 1877 America, the existence of markets does not tell us much at all. But the nature of production, and particularly the relation of production to exchange, can tell us a great deal indeed.[7]

Production *for* Markets

This brings us back to an essential point about production in 1877 America, where, quite unlike the economic system in fifteenth-century France, production itself is mainly *production for the market*. Before we can even try to understand the nature of this type of production, and the revolution that it entails in the nature of exchange, we first have to try to make sense of how such a changed relation between production and exchange could come about in the first place. In short, *how is it possible to organize a social order such that (almost) all production is not direct production for the producer (like the serf) or someone the producer is directly linked to (like the lord), but production for strangers— production for "the market," for exchange in general?* More specifically, what changes must be made to a social order so as to bring about this new form of production? Here it is essential to grasp an important historical point: it is not just that France in 1454 did not have a system of production oriented toward market exchange. Rather, the more radical point is that prior to the sixteenth century, no social order had ever been based on a mode of production oriented primarily toward market exchange.

Starting with Chapter 4, and throughout Parts II and III we will analyze, explain, and decipher the particular elements and relations, along with the general forces and tendencies in such a social order. But before we begin that project we must first try to explain the historical appearance of such a social order. How does a capitalist mode of production emerge in history?

Notes

1. Here we again see the untenable equation of "limited natural resources," which will indeed be found in nature, with "scarce economic goods," which can only be produced in society.
2. This essential point raises important questions about what it would mean to *transform* an economic order; it may suggest that attempts to change society by intervening in the realm of exchange are futile, or at least significantly limited.
3. We must emphasize that the rough de jure equality between workers and owners does not tell us anything definitive about the overall equality in the society, nor does it indicate what the de facto relations of power were between workers and owners. In 1877, America was still a deeply unequal society: the end of Reconstruction the year before meant the abandonment of the project to uphold racial equality and the reestablishment of a racial order of domination across the South; and it was still almost half a century before women would win the right to vote. The point here is not to make any absolute evaluations of the state of equality in American society across its history but to compare directly 1877 America with 1454 France and therefore to highlight the stark differences between a mode of production based on legal relations of bondage (serf to lord) versus a mode of production based on legal relations of equality (worker and owner).
4. The more complete formula, as indicated in the parenthetical phrase "a particular amount of," would be better expressed as $xC_o = yC_p$. That is, the peas commodity and the oats commodity are equal only so long as we have the right proportions of each. X and Y represent those proportions, or, in algebraic terms, the coefficients. We will return to this basic formula in detail in Chapter 5.
5. We will return to this possibility in Chapter 3.
6. This hypothetical person who would pay me for my oats is always excluded from textbook accounts of the supposed transition from barter to a money

economy. This person is a *dealer*, who holds inventories of both goods and money so that she can trade in both (she pays me for my oats not because she wants to eat them but so she can trade them). The textbooks follow a functionalist logic, which assumes that because money makes economic transactions more convenient, we must have introduced money historically in order to overcome the inconveniences of barter. But the logic proves faulty: in order for money to be introduced to markets someone must introduce it, *and they will not do so for free*. The oat dealer will only buy my oats if she thinks she can make a *profit* in doing so. We will return to these ideas in the next two chapters; here they provide a hint of what is to come.

7. This relation will prove central to Part III, particularly as we consider the links between the actions and choices of entrepreneurs and the role of investment, a link that will come to define and partially determine the conditions of a capitalist economic order.

3

Capitalist Social Orders

Defining Capitalism

The previous chapters have shown that to distinguish between social orders in economic terms we should look to *production*. The *differences* between economic orders take shape most clearly in this domain. Production is primary because a society with, for example, a feudal mode of production has an entirely different economic system from a society with a different mode of production. Each particular society may include within it markets for exchange, and the two societies may be concretely linked to one another by global networks of trade. Yet the two are clearly distinguishable by the distinct ways in which they organize production. Hence one of our conclusions from the previous chapter: that the presence of markets does not allow us to distinguish one economic order from another.

This deductive logic tells us something very significant: it demonstrates that what makes a *capitalist* social order unique is that it has a *capitalist mode of production*. Given the title of this book, readers should be suspicious about the fact that we have yet to define "capitalism." Shouldn't a clear definition of capitalism have appeared right at the outset? This is a fair question, yet our previous accounts have demonstrated why the answer turns out to be less than simple. "Capitalism" cannot be determined or delineated in purely analytic or logical terms. No abstract definition of capitalism will do because capitalism proves to be an historical phenomenon. It comes to be at a particular time and place in history. Prior to that time it literally does not exist. After its emergence we can surely work out its basic mechanics or terms—and therefore define it in relatively straightforward and boiled-down language. Nonetheless, capitalism itself will always depend on, will always be constitutively enabled by, the continued maintenance of the very historical conditions that made it possible to emerge in the first place.

Capitalist Economics. Samuel A. Chambers, Oxford University Press. © Oxford University Press 2022.
DOI: 10.1093/oso/9780197556887.003.0004

This chapter brings us to the place in the book where we can finally define capitalism for the first time. Crucially, however, we will do so by defining a capitalist social order. *"Capitalism," in the sense of a "capitalist economic system," is nothing more or less than a social order that is organized, structured, and maintained by and through the capitalist mode of production.* This means, rather simply, that the key to understanding capitalism lies in grasping the nature of a capitalist mode of production. This fact has a few crucial implications for the work we will do in this chapter. First, it means that a full *definition* of capitalism will have to wait until we have charted the initial historical appearance of a capitalist social order. Second, it means that we have to maintain a few somewhat fine-grained conceptual and terminological distinctions.

As we develop the argument in this chapter we will clarify and refine the following concepts/terms:

- **Markets**, which we will show (continuing our discussion from the previous chapter) can have both noncapitalist and capitalist uses.
- **The Capitalist Use of Markets**, which must be explained in its own terms, but also carefully distinguished from a capitalist mode of production.
- **The Capitalist Mode of Production**, which depends on a unique relationship between production and exchange while also entailing the following: a radically new relation between labor and ownership; a peculiar distribution of the means of production; and a deep entwinement between money and the entire economic system of production, distribution, exchange, and consumption.
- **A Capitalist Social Order**, which we can define simply as a social order marked by a capitalist mode of production.

The sections that follow will develop these concepts: first by tracking the first historical appearance of capitalism and then by providing our working definition of capitalism, which will guide us throughout the remainder of the book. But from the outset it is crucial to always keep in mind that markets can be used for capitalist and noncapitalist ends; the mere fact that we observe a market used in a "capitalist" manner does not mean that we are witness to a capitalist social order; and the latter only exists where the mode of production (not just the use of markets) is capitalist.

What's a Market Good For?

The previous chapter developed a careful analysis of the use of markets (locations for the free trading of goods and services) in a feudal social order (fifteenth-century France). In a society in which production is not directly related to the market, we can, for heuristic purposes, conceive of the market as a site for the exchange of equivalents. That is, in such a society the market serves mainly as a place for owners of goods to trade equivalent goods with other owners. Such transactions can be represented symbolically as $C \to C$. We also explained, following standard textbook accounts, that money could be introduced as a technical convenience that facilitates this basic market transaction—this gives us $C \to M \to C$.

On the one hand, the second formula (with money) changes nothing at all; fundamentally we still have the substitution of one commodity for a different one, or, from the perspective of a single commodity owner, we have the transformation of one commodity into a new commodity. It's as if my oats were magically turned into peas. That process seems to be the same whether or not we use money as part of the transformation.

On the other hand, this apparently simple addition of money as a mere "convenience" actually turns out to be a bit more complicated than either we made it appear in the last chapter or than most economic textbooks do when they introduce money. The first and primary difference is temporal. That is, the $C \to C$ transaction is singular and instantaneous: I give you oats at the same moment you give me peas. But the $C \to M \to C$ transaction occurs in two stages: first I sell my oats for money; then, some time later, I use the money to buy peas. Once the two-stage process is complete, it looks no different than direct barter, $C \to C$. However, *the introduction of money* and the creation of a two-stage rather than an instantaneous process *makes it possible to separate the stages.*

In other words, rather than a single process of $C \to M \to C$, we now have two distinct components of exchange: $C \to M$ and $M \to C$. Above we just assumed that $C \to M$ comes first and $M \to C$ follows it. However, nothing inherent to either process requires it to appear in that standard sequence. Moreover, nothing in either of the processes requires it be *followed* by the other process *at all*. Each can function independently, without need of the other. In other words, nothing prevents me from selling my oats for money and then going home. And more significantly, nothing prevents the person who bought my oats from buying lots and lots of oats and then leaving the market with them.

This probably seems like a really basic point—an obvious or even banal one. You might wonder why we seem to be making so much of it. Here's why: **the hidden clue to capitalist economics can be found here**, in the fact that the $C \to M \to C$ code involves two separable, independent processes that need not be paired together and need not follow each other in any order.[1] Our base for tracking down that clue (and thus explaining capitalist economics) is this fact: **when we transform our market formula from $C \to C$ to $C \to M \to C$, we make it possible for a market to be used for an entirely different purpose.**

In order to develop this crucial point, recall that we first introduced "the market" in the context of a fifteenth-century feudal order, where the vast majority of goods and services were produced not for exchange but for direct consumption by lords and serfs. The main purpose of the market was to trade for luxury goods or to balance out excess and limited supplies: I might have been bringing oats to market as a representative of the lord from an estate that grew an abundant supply of oats but not very much in the way of peas. I am using the market to turn the extra oats into peas. The market functions in order to exchange equivalents. And if all market transactions consist in the direct swapping of one commodity for another,[2] then the *only* reason to go to a market, to *use* a market, would be to exchange one good for another.

However, if we have a *monetary* form of market exchange, $C \to M \to C$, then we have the potential for something more than the exchange of equivalents. The fact that $C \to M \to C$ breaks down into distinct and independent components ($C \to M$ and $M \to C$) makes it possible to use the market differently. Rather than exchange equivalent commodities, **we can use the market to make money.** How could we do this? There are myriad options:

1. We buy both oats and peas at harvest time, when supply is high and price is low. Then we hold them until supply is lower and sell when the price is higher.
2. We buy *all* the oats or *all* the peas, controlling the market and allowing us to charge much higher prices than we paid.
3. We buy (oats or peas) in one place (with high supply/low price) and sell in a different place (with low supply/high price).
4. We combine 2 and 3 by controlling the trade routes between places with low and high prices.

We could expand this list in a variety of ways, but let's stop here and take stock of this crucial new development. Notice that in all of these examples we are not arriving at market with a commodity (C_1) that we wish to exchange for an equivalent (C_2); we are arriving at the market with money (M). This means that we have reversed the two stages. Rather than $C \rightarrow M \rightarrow C$, our process in all of these examples can be expressed as $M \rightarrow C \rightarrow M$. We begin with money, and in the first stage we buy a commodity, $M \rightarrow C$; then, at a later stage, we sell that commodity for money, $C \rightarrow M$. At first glance it might seem like these two stages are the same as our earlier two stages of trading equivalents, but we need to look more closely at the difference between our two formulas:

$$(A) \, C \rightarrow M \rightarrow C$$

$$(B) \, M \rightarrow C \rightarrow M$$

In formula (A), as we have been saying all along, the first C and the second C are *different commodities*, but they are *equivalent in value*. As we detailed in the previous chapter, the possibility of exchange depends on a relation of equality, $C = C$.

Yet the same cannot possibly be true for formula (B). It would make no sense at all if $M = M$. I come to the market with a specific sum of money; I use it to buy a commodity; and then I sell that commodity for money. There is no way I would do any of this unless the second M was a *greater sum than the initial M*. If they were equivalent, the entire process would have been a colossal waste of my time. Formula (B) therefore differs radically from (A), a difference that we can mark with a subtle updating of our symbols. We must rewrite as follows:

$$(C) \quad M \to C \to M'$$

Here M' designates the increase in the amount of the original M. In other words $M' = M + \Delta M$.[3] When we use a market to make money, we use it for capitalist purposes, and formula (C) provides the symbolic representation of the capitalist use of the market.

To repeat the point we made at the beginning of this chapter: the capitalist use of the market is not equivalent to, or a sufficient condition for, a capitalist social order, but it does provide the key to the emergence of that order.

The Origins of Capitalism

Markets have existed throughout recorded history. Capitalist social orders, in stark contrast, are relatively new. Prior to the first appearance of a specifically capitalist mode of production, markets were primarily used for the basic exchange of equivalents that we have detailed. Nonetheless, in any society with a system of money and markets for trade, there has also existed at least the possibility for what we have now defined as the "capitalist use" of markets. Whenever there are markets and money, there is the opportunity to make money in markets. Nonetheless, as we have also shown, those societies with both money and markets were not themselves "capitalist social orders" because they did not have a capitalist mode of production. Neither the presence of markets nor the existence of money-making in markets is enough to produce a capitalist social order. Many other economic orders have also had money and markets, but capitalism is unique. Our task now is to quickly trace the first historical appearance of capitalism.

Here we can pull together a number of threads that we have developed to this point in the book. The primacy of production tells us that a capitalist social order will be distinguished by a capitalist form of production. Capitalism will have a mode of production utterly distinct from feudalism and earlier modes. We need to follow the clue of a capitalist use of markets but connect it back to production. Capitalism first emerges historically when a system of production develops that is linked to, and substantively shaped by, a specifically capitalist use of markets.

The increased development of the capitalist use of markets is a necessary condition for the emergence of capitalism, because a capitalist mode of production could not have come about if there were not markets being used for money-making. **We will find the first appearance of capitalism when we find the first system of production that has been completely restructured as capitalist production—that is, as production for the market.**

There is a massive historical literature on, and contentious debate about, the "origins" of capitalism. Part of the dispute hinges on whether we search for "capitalism" at the level of global trade or look for it at the level of a domestic society. It is clear that the capitalist use of markets between societies appears before the transformation of any particular society's mode of production. This is very important because this capitalist use of markets provides an enabling condition for the first appearance of a capitalist mode of production. Nonetheless, our focus lies mainly on the latter phenomenon as the first appearance of a *uniquely capitalist social order*.

Such a social order does not first emerge with global trade or the rise of various empires; these come much earlier. And a capitalist social order does not appear with and because of industrialization. Indeed, not only does industrialization emerge later, but also capitalism plays the causal role for industrialization (not the other way around). Nor is capitalism a natural outgrowth of "commercial society"—that is, the gradual increase in commerce—although both sometimes do appear together. Most surprising of all, the origin of capitalism is not an "urban" phenomenon; it does not happen in cities.

Capitalism appears for the first time in the countryside of England, in the sixteenth century. It emerges in and through the dramatic transformation and reorganization of English food production. In England in this time period, for the first time in history, an entire segment of

Commercial Capitalism

Neoclassical economics tends to assume that "capital" is a type of material thing that has existed throughout history (for our contrasting definition of capital, see Chapter 7) and therefore, in a certain sense, so has capitalism. This entire first part of this book has worked against this tendency, striving to situate economics *in* history, and this chapter specifies the location of the first historical emergence of a distinctly capitalist mode of production.

Throughout this book we focus mainly on *capitalist economics* at the level of a specific social order, a country or nation-state. But the force of capital relations is today and has always been a global force. From a wider-angle perspective, we could also analyze the emergence of these global capitalist relations, which appeared historically much earlier than the first appearance of a specifically capitalist social order.

"Commercial capitalism" or "merchant capitalism" can be dated to as early as the twelfth to fourteenth centuries and appeared in many parts of the world—in Byzantium, in Muslim trading societies, in Italian city-states, and elsewhere. Under commercial capitalism the capitalist use of markets grew into systemic practices of commercial trade engaged in by merchants, supported by bankers, and often reshaping vast swaths of the world. In most cases the trade of commercial capitalism was made possible by established trade networks, which were themselves defended or transformed through military conquest. At later moments in history, commercial capitalism was inextricably bound up with imperial and colonial relations of domination.

The relation between commercial capitalism and the origins of a uniquely capitalist social order prove both subtle and important, and can be articulated as follows:

- Merchant capitalism does not necessarily or inevitably lead to the emergence of a capitalist social order.
- The global trade networks and broader market forces established by commercial capitalism do play an important role in the first emergence of a capitalist mode of production.
- The emergence of a capitalist social order retains priority in our analysis because it leads to such significant social, economic, and political transformations (e.g., those we have discussed in depth between feudal France and capitalist America).

production is restructured according to a significantly new principle of organization. Food is produced not for the producers themselves (direct mode of production), not for serfs and lords (feudal), and not for state officials who directly expropriate the product (tributary). Instead, production becomes *production for the market* itself. Food is produced directly *as a commodity*; it is made in order to be sold, and the production process is itself reorganized for this express purpose.[4] This means that the entire system of production is organized and structured with the express intention that output will not be consumed directly, transferred to another power, or traded as an equivalent, but instead sold on the market for profit. This restructuring and radical reorganization of food production gives us, for the first time in history, a capitalist mode of production, because the market itself (and specifically the capitalist use of the market) was the driving and shaping force of production. This had never occurred before.

This transformation does not occur on its own, and it is not created by a single, outside causal force. Such a transformation was made possible by a series of specific changes in other elements of the English social order. These included political transformations (a more centralized state than was typical under feudalism), new laws (particularly those establishing individual property rights), and social changes (particularly around the sizes of property held by landowners).

To oversimplify a very complex historical narrative, we can describe the change in these basic terms: the replacement of *serfs* and *lords* by *tenant farmers* and *landlords*.[5] As we discussed previously, serfs were both legally subservient to lords and directly tied to the land. The feudal mode of production was based on (and itself preserved) those social and legal statuses. In contrast, a "tenant farmer" was legally free and independent; his relation and obligations to the landlord were contractual only. But the other side of this freedom from bondage to a lord was a certain dispossession from the land. While the serf had a specific sort of primordial "right" to the land in the form of his direct bondage to the lord's estate, the farmer has no claim whatsoever on the land other than what he is availed by paying a money rent.[6]

Thus the legal bondage of the serf (and the legal privileges of the lord) under feudalism was eliminated, but something else took its place: the constraints and coercion of the market. Unlike serfs, tenant farmers were doubly constrained by the market. First, their output had to be sold on the market, so a successful crop might lead to oversupply, a drop in prices, and economic failure. But even before this point the tenant farmer had to compete in the market for land leases, to bid to the highest market price to win the right to rent the land that he would then farm.

It is crucial to emphasize that these market pressures did not apply solely to the tenant farmer: the market in land leases came into being because landlords were competing among themselves to rent their lands at the highest market prices—to generate the largest income they could from their land. They abandoned centuries-long traditions of "customary rents" and rents in kind, replacing them with lease values determined by complex (if abstract) calculations of future market value of crops. In English food production in the six-teenth century, the market became a productive and coercive force. Landlords, in competition with other landlords, had every incentive to push rents as high as they could, which in turn forced farmers to maximize productivity (output relative to labor).[7] In other words, the market (exchange) becomes the very center of gravity for pro-duction itself.

Food production in sixteenth-century England is reorganized ac-cording to the imperatives of the market. Production becomes the production not of goods to consume directly but of commodities to sell for profit. This marks the first appearance of a capitalist mode of production.

The Capitalist Mode of Production

We can begin to clarify this conception of capitalism by returning to our symbolic representations of exchange. To grasp the essence of cap-italism we have to see the mutually constitutive entanglement of the supposedly separate realms of production and exchange. Capitalism is that system in which production is organized according to the imperatives of exchange, and production proceeds with exchange as its ultimate goal. While continuing to affirm our general thesis on the primacy of production, capitalism is a mode of production that makes exchange absolutely central.

To bring a capitalist mode of production into sharper focus, we can return to our symbolic code. Indeed, it is possible to schematize capitalist production by augmenting our earlier formulas for market exchange. Here is what capitalism looks like in those symbols:

$$M \to C...P...C' \to M'$$

Notice first of all that the basic outline of this code is the same as the one we developed to depict the capitalist use of markets. If we look only to the left and right sides, blocking out the middle portion (...P...), we are left with only a slightly altered version of our earlier formula, $M \to C \to M'$. This means that fundamentally we are dealing with a process of circulation: we start with money, use it for specific purposes (to buy commodities), and end up with (more) money. Still eliding the middle part, the main difference with the basic formula for exchange is the introduction of C' into the code. Our initial C, the commodity we purchased with money, somehow gets transformed into C', the commodity we sell for money.

The production process effects such a transformation, and we represent it in our code by the symbol P, with the ellipses on each side indicating the necessary temporal aspect of the production process—the fact that production takes time and occurs in what economic thinkers often refer to as a "production period." The specific details and logistics of any particular production process will prove complex and often distinct from any other production process, subtleties that cannot be captured by P but that it represents in generic terms. Once we have this place in our code for the production process itself, we can therefore describe the entire formula for capitalist production. Here is that description, in steps:

1. We must start with money (M). No production process can begin without an agent already being in possession of some amount of money. We assume this here, as we did in the basic formula for capitalist exchange, but as we will see later, especially in Part III, this fact proves crucial.

2. We buy commodities (C). But these are not typical commodities, as we want them neither for our own consumption nor for direct trade. The first C in this formula represents our purchase of everything needed to carry out a production process. C then includes both the *means of production*, the basic materials required for production, and *labor-hours*, the time spent laboring by workers, who constitute part of the production process.

3. Production occurs (...P...). Again, this is the most schematic element of the code. Nonetheless, it helpfully stands in for the process of production itself, the setting into motion of both labor (by workers) and materials, such that at the end we have a finished good, a produced commodity.

4. Production completes, giving us our commodity for sale (C'). Notice that C' is not an augmentation of our original C but a total transformation and creation of something new.

5. We sell our commodity for money, and for profit (M'). The sale of C' brings in revenue greater than our costs, C, such that we complete the process with more money than we started because, as previously defined, $M' = M + \Delta M$.[8]

This formula therefore conveys the broad structure of a capitalist mode of production.

Capitalist Social Orders

As we stated at the outset, the definition of a capitalist social order is nothing other than a society centered on a capitalist mode of production. Of course, "society" is just the general name for a social order, a concept that always includes political and social structures, the particular legal system, and so on. Therefore, in saying that a capitalist social order is a society centered on a capitalist mode of production, we specifically *include* the social/cultural/political forces that make up that social order. Now that we have delineated a capitalist mode of production and described its first historical emergence, we can finally give a more general definition of capitalism.

In a capitalist social order, the capitalist use of the market—the use of the market for money-making—transforms the entire mode of production of society, such that production becomes production for profitable exchange. Under capitalism, most goods and services are produced not for direct consumption by either the producers or those they are closely linked to in society. Instead, even the most basic necessities (food, shelter, clothing) are produced as commodities for sale on the market, and such necessities can only be accessed through the market. This means that under capitalism the market becomes a central gravitational force for the entire social order. In order to live, workers must sell their labor-hours for money. In order to initiate and carry out processes of production, enterprise owners must turn to the market to purchase both means of production and labor-hours. Workers and enterprise owners remain subject to constant market forces and constraints because the capitalist mode of production renders all actors dependent on the market. Therefore a capitalist social order is marked above all by market competition and the imperative of profit maximization.

Notes

1. Here we mean "code" *not* in the sense of secret or hidden message, but in the sense of computer code or algorithms. We are trying to represent in simplified symbolic language the "code" of a capitalist economy—the instruction set that expresses its basic structures, principles, and operations.
2. Note that in the absence of money we are left with market exchange as direct barter, which is what $C \to C$ symbolizes. Without money, a market can only be used for the exchange of equivalents. In Chapter 4 we will touch on the important fact that, in the historical record, barter turns out to be much rarer than often imagined by texts in economics. More significantly, the practice of barter actually appears historically only *after* the widespread use of money. This means that our conceptual account of the difference between barter, $C \to C$, and money exchange, $C \to M \to C$, is absolutely not an historical account. The difference between these two formulas still holds validity, and it proves critical for our analysis of the uses of markets. But that conceptual analysis should not be transposed or projected onto history to

suggest that the use of money emerges out of earlier practices of barter. That never happened.

3. The Greek letter *delta*, Δ, represents a *change* in quantity.

4. Obviously there were earlier moments in time when goods were produced in order to be sold, but capitalism in the sense of a capitalist social order only comes about when the system of production is transformed according to this principle.

5. Technically the term "tenant farmer" is redundant since the earliest meanings of the English word "farmer" (dating to the fifteenth century) include "lessee," "renter," and "one who rents land for the purpose of cultivation."

6. "Money rent" may sound redundant to twenty-first-century ears since we always pay rents in money. But in feudalism, and even for long periods of transition to a capitalist mode of production, rents were often paid "in kind"; this means that the "rent" was a portion of the produced output itself, e.g., "corn rent." Even within developed capitalist social orders, rents in kind can persist and even grow, as they did throughout much of the American South for more than half a century after the Civil War, in the form of sharecropping.

7. We will return to the key concept of productivity in Parts II and III of this book, but it should be noted here that the emergence of a capitalist mode of production in English food production in the sixteenth century helps to explain why by the seventeenth century, productivity in farming is so much higher in England—compared, for example, with still-feudal France.

8. Close readers will notice that in the code for capitalist production, ΔM seems to reflect an implicit ΔC. In other words, M' is larger than M precisely because C' sells for more than we paid for C. We will return to a close scrutiny of these issues in Chapter 6.

PART II

CAPITALIST ECONOMIC RELATIONS

Part I situated the question of economic forces and relations in both social and historical context. It showed that economic forces never operate in isolation; they can only exist within concrete social formations, which are themselves constituted by hierarchical power relations. Those social and political structures of power form the background for economic forces. For example, because a feudal society is populated by lords and serfs, economic forces under feudalism look utterly different than economics in a liberal civil society in which there literally are no such things as lords and serfs. This means that the economic cannot be studied abstractly; it can only be grasped as an element and a logic within a specific, and specifically defined, social formation.

Moreover, Part I demonstrated that social orders develop, change, and transmute over time—that is, within history. Economic relations are historical relations that cannot be excised from temporal movements. Chapter 3 explored the historical emergence of a capitalist mode of production—a capitalist social order. The transformation of social, legal, and property relations—starting in England in the sixteenth century—led to the reorganization of large parts of society's production of goods. For the first time in history, large swaths of societal production were rearranged for an entirely new set of ends or purposes. This brought into prominence the force of capital, which we described through the code whereby money is used to produce commodities for the express purpose of selling those same commodities for profit.

In Part II we pivot and zoom in. We pivot away from historical analysis toward a more abstract and analytical attempt to study the economic forces and relations that operate in a capitalist social formation. We zoom in on precisely those key elements that make up the central core of economics within a capitalist social order, thereby leaving the historical analysis behind (for now). Each chapter of Part II therefore focuses directly on one such element: money (Chapter 4), commodities (Chapter 5), and profit (Chapter 6). This means that we will be analyzing in detail, and in sequence, each element in the formula for the capitalist use of markets: $M \rightarrow C \rightarrow M'$.

We must constantly keep in mind, however, that this zoomed-in approach means that everything explained and unpacked in Part II exists *within the context of a capitalist social order*. If at any point while discussing money, commodities, and exchange we were to pan out, the camera would always reveal that we were located in a capitalist society. We would find the elements under study to be situated within a social order organized by and according to the terms of capitalist production. Whereas Part I contains material that almost never makes an appearance in even the longest economics textbooks, Part II addresses more traditional material from economics. At the outset then, we should underscore a few key differences.

1. We *start* with money. Whereas most analyses either exclude money entirely or relegate it to an ancillary role, we emphasize that money is an economic force, and that all economic relations take the form of monetary relations. There is no possibility of "bracketing" money from the analysis, and there is no such thing as a "real economy" separate from money.

2. Each chapter centers on one key element or relation, but each of these elements remains bound up with and constantly presupposes and implies the others. Commodities, money, and profit cannot appear in isolation from one another; none "comes first" in the logical analysis, even though we have no choice but to present one prior to the others in the running chapter order. The order of the chapters should not be taken to reflect any kind of logical or historical priority of concepts. Partially in an effort to drive this point home, we start with money (the element

so often excluded or marginalized by traditional approaches), but this does not mean that money exists first. There cannot be money without economic activity, which often takes the form of exchange of commodities. None of these elements can exist without the others.

3. Because capitalism provides the background for the analysis of these core concepts, each element is marked by and depends on the code of capital—even as our study of these elements is what will make it possible to grasp more precisely how that code works (in Part III). In other words, though these chapters take a *more abstract* approach, this does not mean that they offer an *ahistorical* analysis. We will be concerned here with the nature of money, commodities, and profit as they exist and operate under capitalism. Other, noncapitalist, social formations had trade, and thereby *exchanged* goods and services; money predates the emergence of capitalism by thousands of years; and the limited sense of profit as *net revenue* does not depend on a capitalist mode of production. However, money and profit under capitalism take on unique and crucially important properties, which it will be our task in Part II to unpack and grasp. Finally, according to the specific and precise conceptualization of commodities that we provide here, strictly speaking, the commodity only comes to exist within a capitalist social order. This does not preclude or deny the fact that goods have been produced, traded, and sold for money (and even for a kind of profit) prior to capitalism. Nonetheless, we will show that the nature of the capitalist commodity is unique to capitalism, and this has enormous implications for a wide array of economic forces and relations.

In any case, it proves impossible to grasp the complex nature of the capitalist commodity without first trying to make sense out of an element equally complex and mysterious—namely, money.

4

Money

Money seems like it ought to be easy enough to understand. Money surrounds us all, and we use it every single day. Unlike a whole host of complicated and arcane financial devices (from bonds to derivatives to credit default swaps), money is practical and uncomplicated. We learn how to spend money more easily than we learn a language, so money shouldn't be so hard. Indeed, we might assume that we all already know the language of money because we are fluent in its practical use. What more is there to learn? And as we have already covered, many standard treatments of economics approach money in just this way: they define money simply as the "means of exchange" and use the metaphor of "lubricant" to describe the simplicity of money as a technical device that aids us in buying and selling things.

If only it were that easy. Unfortunately, it turns out that money is hard—really hard. John Maynard Keynes was arguably the greatest economist of the twentieth century, but early in his career he spent the better part of a decade trying to come to terms with the theory and history of money. Keynes referred to this period as his "Babylonian madness" because trying to grasp the nature of money (through study of the ancient Babylonians) drove Keynes close to insanity. Closer to our own time period, Geoffrey Ingham may be the single most important authority on money today, but he only arrived at that point through his own form of Babylonian madness. Ingham is a sociologist who contracted to write a short introductory sociology text on economic institutions. His first chapter, like this one, was meant to provide a brief discussion of money. But instead of writing that chapter and that book, Ingham delivered a different book, and delivered it many years late—an entire book on money (Ingham 2004). All in all, Ingham has now spent at least a quarter of a century trying to understand money.

Obviously we don't have that long. But we can move more quickly if we remind ourselves that just because we can use a technology does

Capitalist Economics. Samuel A. Chambers, Oxford University Press. © Oxford University Press 2022.
DOI: 10.1093/oso/9780197556887.003.0005

not mean that we understand its nature—just because something is central to our lives doesn't mean it's simple. The computer I'm typing on—today and every day—is made up of solid-state transistors, themselves only made possible by the theory of quantum mechanics. But using my computer daily puts me no closer to grasping quantum mechanics, a field so complex that most physicists don't even understand it. Hence our starting point in tackling money depends on refusing the idea that it is simple just because our use of it seems straightforward.

The Paradox of Money

A deep understanding of money requires grasping it as fully paradoxical. Money is a paradox because of two simultaneous truths about it:

1. Money is not what it seems.
   As we will explore in greater detail in this chapter, in our practical experience and daily use of money, it appears to be something other than what it truly is. In this sense, money is like the pencil submerged in water, which appears to us as bent, though it is in fact straight.
2. What money is depends on what it seems to be.
   Money is not an illusion; **money is a paradox**. In order to understand money we have to grasp its paradoxical nature. Having shown that money is not what it seems, we will demonstrate that money's distorted appearance is necessary, fundamental, and an essential element of its very nature. In this sense, money is nothing like the pencil submerged in water. The "stick in water" case provides a classic example of *illusion*: the pencil appears bent, but there is nothing about the pencil that partakes of "bentness," so its appearance proves totally false. The nature of money within capitalism turns out to be quite different from this standard example: *appearing to be other than it is proves essential to money's very nature*. Pencils appear to be straight most of the time; only when we submerge part of them in water—due to the properties of light refraction through different media—do they appear bent. To make the pencil analogy hold, we would have to

find a type of straight pencil that always appeared bent. Money would then be like that object: it always appears to be other than it is, and therefore its appearing as other actually forms a key part of its very nature. If money is not illusion but paradox, then in order to understand money we must grasp its paradoxical nature.

We will now develop each of these points in detail.

Money Is Not What It Seems

When we encounter and use money in our daily lives within a capitalist society, money seems like the very incarnation of economic value—value in its purest form. Any economics textbook will tell you that "money is the medium of exchange," meaning simply that if you have money, you can "trade it" for commodities. This definition says that money is the "stuff" you use to get the "stuff" you want, and since money is a *universal* means of payment and means of exchange—that is, you can use it to pay for *any* goods or services, to cancel *any* debt or obligation—money thus becomes, in an important sense, the highest form of value. And most of us, most of the time, would prefer to hold value in the form of money. For example, if I offer you the choice of either (a) five iPhones, each with a market value of $1,000, or (b) $5,000, you are almost certainly going to choose option (b). Indeed, the only conditions under which you might choose (a) would be if for some reason you knew of a set of market conditions that would allow you to exchange the five iPhones for an amount of money greater than $5,000. This exception would therefore prove the general rule since in both cases you will prefer the larger amount of value as measured in money terms. You would only choose commodities over money if the commodities were "worth more," but the measure of their worth is always itself a monetary measure. Even if you chose to hold the commodities for a short period of time, you would be valuing them in terms of money. And in order to *realize* the exchange-value of the commodities, you would need to swap them for money. *Within a capitalist society, value appears in the form of money, while money appears to be value.*

All of this means that money seems to be the positive, substantive manifestation of value itself. Money appears to have a direct, intrinsic value. Movies repeatedly illustrate this point with stories that pivot around the search for, or loss of, a massive sum of money. In almost every case the director makes certain to *show us the money*—usually in the shape of briefcases or duffle bags full of cash, but sometimes in the form of account numbers and balances on a computer screen. The point holds in either case: money appears as the manifestation of positive, intrinsic value. As we encounter money in our daily lives, it repeatedly seems to us that by "having" money, we thereby *hold or possess value*. This notion feels intuitively correct to us, and the orthodox theory of money, a key tenet of modern economics, supports this idea of money.

Dollars and Bricks

Nevertheless, money is not what it seems, and this conceptualization of money as positive, intrinsic value turns out to be false.[1] To understand why the intuitive idea of money as possessable value is wrong, we can start by seeing that "money" is not a concrete material object, or even a singular entity. In other words, there is no such thing as money in itself, in isolation, or as an elemental particle.

A shoe and a brick are both empirical objects that we can hold, view, and measure. Each has a specific use, and each can have a size, weight, and shape. When placed on scales we may find that the shoe weighs 300 grams and the brick weighs 2 kilograms. We could use a tape measure to generate similar numbers for length, width, and height. But in addition to their physical uses and their physical parameters, both a shoe and a brick may also have exchange-values, market values—that is, prices. Let's say the shoe has a value/price of $50, whereas the brick has a value/price of $0.50. Notice what has occurred here: while we are still focusing on the nature of two empirical objects, two commodities, we have now introduced "dollars," and therefore we have tacitly introduced money. One way to ask the question "What is money?" would be to rephrase it in the form of the question "*What is a dollar?*"

As this example makes clear, the dollar is a *measure of value* in the same way that grams are a measure of weight and meters are a measure of length. The analogy can be extended in important ways:

1. Just as we can have multiple measures of weight, such as grams and pounds, we can have multiple measures of value, such as dollars and euros.
2. Just as a meaningful comparison of length (e.g., which shoe is bigger?) requires us to measure in the same units (e.g., inches), a meaningful comparison of value/price (which brick is worth/costs more?) requires us to measure value in the same monetary units (e.g., rupees).
3. Just as we can *convert* from one unit of measurement of weight to another (1 kg = 2.2 lbs.), we can also *convert* from one unit of measurement of value/price to another (1 euro = 77 rupees).

Notice, of course, that the analogy has crucial limits, and that the relation is *disanalogous* in important ways:

A. Assuming no event alters the physical brick itself, we conclude that it *always* weighs 2 kilograms, but the value/price of the brick might be $0.50 today and $0.45 tomorrow. Even though money is the measure of value, the value of the entity that it measures can change (sometimes rapidly and severely) without any physical change occurring. Indeed, **while money is a measure of value, what it measures (value/price) is not itself a physical property.**
B. The conversion between different measures of length and weight do not alter—1 inch always equals 2.54 centimeters—but the exchange rates between different measures of value change all the time—today 1 dollar equals 19 pesos, but tomorrow it might equal 18 or 20 pesos.

Therefore we can conclude that the dollar (and money in general) is a measure of value both like and unlike the meter is a measure of length. The key to seeing why our intuitive grasp of money as the incarnation of intrinsic value proves to be wrong can be found in the bolded sentence in point A. Money measures value, but value itself is not the property of any object, any "thing" at all. Money tends to deceive us, partially because we think we can hold it in our hand just like the shoe or the brick, when in reality money is much more like the meter than the brick. A. Mitchell Innes, one of the first to write perspicaciously about the paradoxical nature of money, put the point this way: "The eye has never seen, nor the hand touched a dollar" (Innes 1914: 155). This radical claim makes a lot of sense now that we have already seen the similarities between a dollar and an inch—no one would ever claim that they had touched or held "47 inches."

What Is Money?

But what, then, is a dollar? And how do we make sense of ubiquitous claims to have or hold dollars in just the sense that Innes says is impossible? The examples are utterly commonplace: "I'll give you $20 to cover my portion of the meal"; "Jeff Bezos has $175 billion." These claims sound to us nothing like the ridiculous statement "I have 4 centimeters." Yet Innes has suggested that, in point of fact, "I have $20" in the sense that I possess and hold it directly is as nonsensical as "I have 47 inches."

We might try to overcome this problem by dismissing it as a linguistic oddity. Hence we could say that the claim to "hold dollars" is really a claim to hold objects (commodities) that are worth that much when measured in dollars. The technically false claim to hold a dollar in our hands would just be a quirk of language that applies only to money. That is, if I have a brick in my hand, I say that it *weighs* 5 pounds, but I don't say I am in possession of 5 pounds. However, when I hold money in my hand, rather than saying the money is *worth* 5 dollars, I simply say, "I have 5 dollars."

But this effort fails; it cannot solve the riddle of "holding dollars." The reason is that the parallel will not hold. It's true that if I have a brick in my hand, I can say that its measure of weight is 5 pounds and its measure of worth is $0.50. Hence in a certain sense I might be thought to "have $0.50" because I have a physical object that is worth

$0.50. But this is cheating: we know that there is a big difference between possessing commodities with ideal values (prices) in money, and possessing the money itself. I could own 2 tons of bricks, valued today at $1,000, but this is in no way the same as holding $1,000. And the reason is obvious: tomorrow the price of bricks might drop to $0.25, and I would only be able to sell my 2 tons for $500. Perhaps the bricks are made in China and I plan to sell them to US companies, but tomorrow the US government announces a new tariff on Chinese imports, making the cost of bricks much higher for my potential customers; they will therefore not pay me as much tomorrow as they would have yesterday.

The comparison cannot be between the measure of the brick in pounds and the measure of the brick in dollars because the question is about the nature of the dollar, of money, itself. When I say, "I have $20," I am explicitly not saying that I have goods and services that I might, potentially, sell in the future for $20; I am saying that I have a $20 bill, or a bank account with $20 in it. Innes's claim turns out to be even more radical than it may have first appeared: in addition to suggesting that dollars are like meters (both are *measures*, not material objects), he is also saying that even when you have a $20 bill in your hand, you still do not directly possess $20 of value.

What, then, is a $20 bill or a £5 note? What is money *in itself*—that is, apart from its existence as a measure of value of other things?

Money Is Credit/Debt

We might find a clue to the nature of money by looking at the US $20 bill or the UK £5 note. On the top of the latter, we find these words: "Bank of England / I promise to pay the bearer on demand the sum of Five Pounds" (see Lanchester 2016). The paradox of money flashes here, written down for all the world to see, since in one sense these words make no sense whatsoever. The £5 note states that its possessor can exchange it for £5. But if I already have £5, why would I want to swap it for £5? *What would that even mean?* And if possessing a £5 note only guarantees that I can swap it for a £5 note, then what is a £5 note to begin with? We seem not to have answered the question, "What's £5?"

Perhaps the writing on the $20 bill can clear things up. There we find these words: "This note is legal tender for all debts, public and private." The $20 bill defines money as *legal tender*, a technical term for that which is accorded legal status as an instrument capable of extinguishing debt. Money is the thing that allows you to pay off debt. Moreover, as Innes explained clearly more than a century ago, "a credit redeems a debt and nothing else does" (Innes 1914: 154).[2] In other words, **money is credit**. This means that when we buy or sell, we do not actually exchange one commodity for another commodity. Rather, we exchange a commodity for a credit; "credit and credit alone is money" (Innes 1913: 392). In this context, we must emphasize that credit and debt are opposite sides of the same coin. If you owe me, then I have a credit and you have a debt. **To have money means to have a credit with some other entity that recognizes that credit**, and thereby acknowledges their debt to you. This means that money is always both an asset for one person and a liability for someone else.

One powerful way to explain this key insight is by rethinking the relationship between banks and account holders. The intuitive understanding of money as positive, intrinsic value fits neatly into a standard narrative in which banks play the role of safeguarding "our" money. This story conceives of banks as "intermediaries" between "savers," who deposit *their* money, and "borrowers," to whom the bank lends that same money out. In his first book, Keynes absolutely exploded this myth of banks as intermediaries, and yet it still persists in orthodox economic accounts. The central problem with such a narrative is that it assumes that money is like iPhones, a commodity possessing intrinsic value that we then hand over to the bank to hold on our behalf. My iPhone is an asset for me, but a liability for no one; it is a commodity, not money.

In actual fact, a deposit account is not the site of positive money— an entity that the bank would "hold" (in the sense of possessing) on my behalf—but a credit we "hold" (in the sense of wielding) against the bank. If we "deposit" money, we make our bank a debtor to us. For example, if I have a checking account with Citibank with a balance of $300, then $300 is the amount of credit I have. Citibank is my debtor; *they owe me* that $300. Indeed, we tend to assume that the bank possesses our money, but the reality turns out to be just the opposite: as every banker knows, deposit accounts are listed as *liabilities* on the balance sheet of a bank. Importantly, but for most, counterintuitively, *loans are a bank's primary monetary assets.*[3] To repeat, money is credit/ debt. So when the bank loans us money, we become debtors to the bank, and it gains a credit. Moreover, the inception of the loan is itself *money creation*, as it creates a new asset and liability for the bank, and a new asset and liability for us. This also means that when we deposit money into a bank account, we merely *transfer a credit* from elsewhere, swapping one debtor for another.

By shedding light on banking practices—that is, by understanding deposits as customer credits (bank debts) and loans as bank assets (customer debts)—we can also make more sense out of what often appears to be the most concrete form of money, *cash*. **Coins and notes are credits against the government itself.** Hence we can answer the riddle written on the £5 note: to "pay the bearer the sum of £5" means that the Bank of England is the *debtor*, and whoever holds the bill holds a *credit* of £5 against the UK government. Innes put it best in his original formulation of the credit theory of money: "A first-class credit is the most valuable kind of property" (Innes 1913: 392). Money cannot be "sound" in the sense of resting on any sort of intrinsic value; **money is always social, and always relational, because it always involves two parties and a relation to the future** (for repayment of debt). Yet money can surely be more or less sound depending on the quality of the debtor. When, in a recent report, Credit Suisse outlines the importance of so-called "high quality liquid assets," they are echoing Innes one hundred years later. The fundamental point, both then and now, is that everyone wants much of their money (i.e., their credit) to be held on the most trustworthy debtor. Today that often takes the form of US Treasury bonds.[4] Money is always a credit held somewhere, a debt owed by someone, and thus we would always prefer to have the most trustworthy debtor. In the case of notes and coins, that debtor is the government itself. As an added benefit, one can always use notes and coins to pay off debts owed to the government itself (i.e., taxes).[5]

Money Is Not a Commodity

We are therefore drawn naturally and logically (if also fitfully) to the conclusion that money is not what it seems: money is not a commodity, and money is not positive, intrinsic economic value. Money is credit/debt, which means **money only exists as a set of social (and often political) relations—relations of trust and reciprocity.** Money only comes into being in social contexts in which one party proves willing to *extend credit* to another party. This, incidentally, helps explain why the only historical instances of the barter of commodities appear *between* cultures foreign to one another, between societies that do not know and do not trust one another. Practices of barter mark not the *origin* of money but its *absence*. In the anthropological record, barter only emerges *after* the appearance of money as credit. Bartering is not what a society did before it invented money; bartering is what two different money societies do when they need to conduct economic transactions in the absence of a *common* money (which is not the same thing as a shortage of cash).

Most importantly, credit is not based on or backed by a primary, intrinsic value; credit is not an "extension" of a prior money as a medium of exchange. Rather, credit comes first; the credit relation is precisely the fundamental money relation. Money never exists as substantive, positive, or intrinsic value, but only ever as a social relation of credit/debt. As we will explore in more detail in Chapter 8, the fact that money is always credit—a claim against some other party—means that money is never "sound"; money as value is always at risk. We therefore reach the conclusion that money is not at all what we think it is.

Money Is Neither Illusion nor Convention

Nevertheless, money is not just an illusion. We will now begin to illustrate and analyze why money's *appearance*—as positive, intrinsic value—proves to be something much more than false or wrong. To understand money deeply we cannot merely ignore or dismiss these appearances, for while they do not tell us everything we need to know about money, they do tell us something; they are neither "fake" nor nonsense. Here we will try to show how money's *appearance* as positive, intrinsic value actually reveals something very important—not only about money but also about a capitalist social order. Our hypothesis: what money *appears* to be proves central to its function, its social role, its *nature* as money.

In order to unpack and develop the logic that will substantiate such a claim, we need to start by seeing that the conclusion that money is not what it seems has led to two distinct, but similarly unhelpful, responses. First, some scholars of sociology and anthropology have suggested that money be comprehended as nothing other than a set of *sociocultural conventions*. Money, these scholars suggest, may prove important in telling us something about the meaning-making practices within a particular society, but the study of such practices can be effectively prosecuted quite separately from the analysis of the systems of production, distribution, and exchange of those societies (i.e., economics). On these accounts, money is certainly real, but its reality consists solely in a set of cultural practices, very much akin to practices of religion, sport, art, and so on. Indeed, this approach extends the argument that money is not what it seems by claiming that money "really is" nothing more than a set of cultural practices.

In a contrasting yet complementary move, some scholars of economics have argued that money must be understood as nothing more than a *mere economic convention*. According to these thinkers, money is simply an abstract *representation* of economic value, a symbol of real value—where the latter always takes the form of concrete commodities with intrinsic value. The idea of money as ancillary, as *purely symbolic*, helps to explain why almost all introductory economics textbooks have almost nothing to say about money. These texts, like much of modern economic thought, treat money as largely superfluous; they distinguish between, on the one hand, the "real economy," which concerns the production and exchange of commodities, and, on the other hand, "monetary" concerns, which can be ignored. Milton Friedman famously argued that money had no *real* effects on the "real economy." For Friedman, money must be understood as no more than a "veil" that stands between us and the *real* economy (and sometimes blocks our vision of the latter). Moreover, Friedman understood money as a "*neutral* veil," not one that hides or distorts. Put simply, this line of reasoning leads straight to the conclusion that money just does not matter that much to modern economics—hence its predominant exclusion from introductory texts.

Both approaches effectively sever money from the fundamental elements of economic activity. The sociological approach studies money practices as rituals almost entirely distinct from economic activity; the economic approach studies economics almost entirely without the presence or importance of money.

Money Is the Point of Capitalist Production

To demonstrate the critical significance of money's appearance (as positive, intrinsic value), we must start with the fact that within a society shaped by the logic of capital, *economic forces and relations are, by definition, monetary*. In other words, the phrase "monetary economy" is redundant. This means that concrete economic practices (e.g., of production and exchange) in a capitalist society are *money practices*, and there is therefore no way to separate the so-called real economy from money. Money is very much real.

This fact proves plain to just about anyone who lives in a capitalist society and pays attention to how things work, because **under the terms of capitalism, the goal is money itself.** We already expressed this point lucidly in our code for capitalist production:

$$M \rightarrow C...P...C' \rightarrow M'$$

This code begins and ends with money; commodities, and even the production process itself, turn out to be intermediaries within a process driven by money. We can state the same point in practical terms. In a capitalist social order, workers take jobs in order to earn wages in money. Business owners and entrepreneurs engage in their ventures in the hope that they will bring in profit, which obviously takes the form of money. Investors put their money into various classes of investment vehicles for the express purpose of gaining more money. We can see the specificity of this capitalist code if we focus on the precise nature of the *production* of commodities. Take, for example, the production of shoes.

If we travel back in time to observe the practices of a Native American tribe, we will see that some members had the skills and devoted the time to sewing leather (a "raw material" acquired by other members of the tribe[6]) into shoes. The goal of this process of production was to produce enough shoes to shod the feet of the tribe's members, and perhaps to have a few pairs of shoes or some raw materials left over in case someone's shoes were lost or worn out. The goal or endpoint for shoe production was ... shoes to wear.

Now let us move forward in time to the present, to a Nike shoe factory in Vietnam. The question of how many shoes to produce, of the systems used to produce them, and even of the location of the factory—all of this falls under the general category of producing shoes to sell on the market for money. Capitalist production is production of goods not for their direct uses but for their exchange-value, which can only be realized in *money*. In other words, the aim of capitalist production is exchange-value (the *price* of the commodity), which can only be realized through the *sale* of the commodity. Stating it directly almost feels vapid, but we need to underscore that the goal of capitalist production is *not* actually the goods themselves; the goal is the money for which they can be sold. The needs of the larger society in terms of shoes to wear are only an indirect concern in the larger calculus of price and profit. If shoe collectors in Los Angeles are willing to buy hundreds of pairs of basketball shoes to stack in their closets, then the shoe factory may produce far more shoes than anyone "needs" in terms of protecting their feet. And if the demand for shoes dries up for some reason, we may find the producer of a commodity destroying the very goods they produced.

The takeaway point here concerns the close relationship, under capitalism, between money and commodities. Where both sociologists and most economists think it possible to sever "economic concerns" from "money matters," we can see clearly, and in contrast, that the nature of capitalist *production* (the engine of economic activity) entails an intrinsic and indissociable *link* between money and commodities. Capitalism is the production of commodities for the realization of value in the form of money.

Capitalism Posits Money as Value Itself

And this returns us to where we started. We can now begin to explain how and why we instinctively believe that money is the very incarnation of positive, intrinsic value. We are drawn to believe such a thing not because of human nature (humans are *not* creatures inherently drawn to money) and not because of the nature of money in and of itself (there is nothing in the physical existence of a dollar bill that tells us it possesses intrinsic value). Instead, we come to believe that *money is value* precisely **because we live in a capitalist social order—** that is, we live in a society shaped and governed by the rules of capital, a society in which economic value takes the form of money. In other words, and as we saw in the first section of this chapter, when analyzed closely we see that money is not literally the positive incarnation of value, and yet, within a society structured by the logic of capital, *economic value does take the form of money*. Capitalism itself depends on, just as it also brings about, the idea of *money as value*.

Money's functional existence in a capitalist society therefore remains entangled with the (false) notion that money *is* positive, intrinsic value. What money is depends on what it seems to be. Some have described this as the "fetish character" of money, meaning that we treat money *as if* it were value itself. Crucially, this fetish character of money arises not because of a mistake that we make in our dealings with money; it arises because of the very nature of capitalist money.[7] Money really does take on this character because of the relationship between money and commodities *as established by* the structure of capitalist production. In other words, within a society in which all production has been organized in order to use money to produce goods to sell and in turn garner more money, in a society in which all basic human needs (food and shelter) can only be met by purchasing goods with money, it is not surprising that people would come to think of money as having intrinsic, positive value.

Close analysis has therefore shown us that money is a social relation of credit/debt. Money is the abstract *measure* of value, but money has no value itself. Nevertheless, money consistently and continually appears within a capitalist society as if it were value itself, since money is the ultimate and most practical form that value can take. Yet money is not necessarily the primary form that value takes within capitalism, and it is surely not the only form. Indeed, many economic writers have argued from a variety of perspectives that the fundamental element of (capitalist) economics is the commodity. In the next chapter we therefore turn to the commodity, but we will find that in doing so we cannot leave money behind.

Notes

1. It's tempting to think that the intuitive, orthodox account of money as positive, intrinsic value was once true. This is the belief that in the past, money was "sound money," constituted by commodities like gold, which did have intrinsic value. However, a close look at the historical record proves this to be false: money, even when it took the form of gold and silver, was always a token, a marker or measure of value, but never value itself. Later in this chapter and then in the next, we will see that when gold and silver function as money, they cease to function as commodities (and vice versa).

2. There may be unusual circumstances in which an explicit law has been passed rendering certain commodities legal tender, or two parties may enter into a contract that specifies a debt measured in certain commodities or services, but these are exceptions to the general rule that money, not commodities, cancels debt.

3. In addition to loans, commercial banks have their own "deposit accounts" in the form of central bank reserves. That is, the central bank is the *banker's bank*, and commercial banks thus have credits on the central bank. We will discuss these points in greater detail in Chapter 8.

4. Hence we can quickly explain one contemporary phenomenon that has frustrated and confused many recent commentators: negative-interest-rate bonds. Put simply, if the creditor seems trustworthy enough, you will *pay them* to be your debtor, i.e., in order to have the right to hold a credit against them.

5. In modern economies, circulating cash is almost always circulating government debt. The so-called state theory of money emphasizes this point, sometimes to insist that sovereign governments can never run out of money because they can continue to issue IOUs that people will accept, precisely because state debt is the ultimate form of money. However, prior to and alongside government debt, we find other forms of circulating credit and debt instruments. This means that the *state theory* of money depends on a broader *credit theory* of money, as described in this chapter. Both historically and today there have been numerous forms of money (of circulating credit/debt) that were distinct from government debt.

6. As part of the production process, the term "raw material" has a precise and counterintuitive economic meaning. "Raw materials" are *inputs* for the production process: they are the original "C" in our code for capitalist production. But this means that "raw materials" are not just found in nature; rather, they are often the product of a previous production process. In the shoe example, leather is not found in nature but must be produced first by hunting and killing an animal, then removing and tanning its hide.

7. As David McNally details, the very concept of the "fetish object" first arose in history when seventeenth-century British colonial traders in Africa found that some members of local African tribes refused to exchange certain objects for British money. The tribespeople saw no intrinsic value in the money—an utterly reasonable and rational response by people who did not live in social orders governed by the rules of capitalism. Unable to process this choice, the colonists explained it by attributing to the Africans a set of mystical beliefs and practices and by inventing the word "fetish" to describe the objects that the tribespeople refused to trade. The British traders couldn't grasp that by assuming money was intrinsically valuable, *it was they who were being weird.* Hence they projected that strangeness onto the African tribes, attributing to them a "fetishism" about certain objects, an *irrational* commitment or devotion to the object. This all arose because the tribespeople refused to treat these objects as commodities, as entities that could always be exchanged for money. This chapter has shown that the true fetish character belongs to capitalist money and capitalist commodities because the social relations of capitalism mean that those entities seem to have the mystical property of intrinsic value (see David McNally 2011).

5

Commodities

This chapter focuses intently on the definition of the "commodity," as we try to understand the precise nature and structure of commodities within a capitalist social order. Capitalism is a system of *circulation*; it circulates money and commodities. In this circulatory system, money is like blood plasma, the purely liquid component that moves other elements through the body; commodities are like blood cells, with a static form, a cellular structure. Commodities are transported through the system by money, but the overall system of circulation depends on the form and role of commodities. Human blood is made up of both plasma and blood cells, and with the naked eye it proves impossible to distinguish between plasma and blood cells. Similarly, the blood of a capitalist social order is constituted by money and commodities, and at times each appears in the shape or form of the other—sometimes we treat money as if it were a commodity, and often commodities act like money. To understand how this is possible, **we need to take a microscope to commodities**—to view their cellular structure. Only then will it be possible (in later chapters) to explore their relation to money, link them to the fundamental question of profit, and explain their central role in a capitalist social order.

This book has already said a great deal about commodities, and a short rehearsal of what we have covered can serve as a point of departure for our deeper analysis of the commodity in this chapter. Right from the start, in Chapter 1, the definition and role of commodities was already at stake. Recall one of the primary problems with Robinsonades: they posit natural resources (literally, physical material found in nature) *as commodities*. In other words, the state-of-nature story implies that we will find *commodities* in nature itself, just lying around. One of our tasks in this chapter is to mark clearly the differences between, on the one hand, a natural resource (water in a lake) or physical good (a table you built for your room) and, on the

Capitalist Economics. Samuel A. Chambers, Oxford University Press. © Oxford University Press 2022.
DOI: 10.1093/oso/9780197556887.003.0006

other, a *capitalist commodity*, which we will define in a more precise and technical sense as a **produced** good/resource/service—produced for the market, created for exchange at a profit.

In Chapter 2 we explored the different relations between commodities and money brought about by distinct uses of market exchange. In basic exchange, money serves as an intermediary, helping to transform one commodity into its equivalent, $C \rightarrow M \rightarrow C$, whereas in the capitalist use of exchange, commodities serve as an intermediary, helping to transform an initial sum of money into a larger sum, $M \rightarrow C \rightarrow M'$. As defined in Chapter 3, a capitalist social order is one distinguished by a capitalist mode of production. Such a mode of production revolves around the commodity: capitalism is the production of commodities not only for exchange but also for sale *at a profit*. Hence our algorithm for capitalism: $M \rightarrow C...P...C' \rightarrow M'$. As we can clearly see, production itself provides the fulcrum for this system, but commodities serve as the two sides of the lever: *production begins with commodities* (raw materials) and *ends with commodities* (finished goods). **A capitalist mode of production is a system of commodity production** wherein the totality of production has been organized and structured with the aim of producing goods for sale at a profit.[1]

Absent Definitions

But what, then, is a commodity? This is our primary question in this chapter, and it would seem as if it should have been a primary question throughout the history of economics. Unfortunately for our purposes, that is not the case; indeed, most economics writers offer no definition of the commodity whatsoever. Modern economics textbooks use the word more or less frequently, but even very long books (filled with definitions of other terms) offer no definition at all of *commodity*. Some figures in classical political economy do devote more time and attention to conceptualizing the commodity, but the treatment of the term by some of the most famous thinkers proves surprising. In his *Principles of Political Economy* (1817), a text thought by many to be the pinnacle of classical political economy, David Ricardo does not even use the word "commodity." In *The Wealth of Nations* (1776) Adam

Smith does use the word frequently in the early parts of his text, but, like the modern textbooks, he does not define it.

What explains these absent definitions of an idea and object that proves so central to economic relations and forces? Perhaps we can find an answer by first consulting the dictionary and then by again considering the Robinsonade. The *Oxford English Dictionary* tells us that the English word "commodity" has both French and Latin origins. The Anglo-Norman and Middle French words from which the English term derives mean both "piece of merchandise" and "profit" (a crucial point to which we will return in Chapter 6). The earliest uses of the word in English, dating from the very end of the fourteenth century, centered on meanings such as "benefit," "interest," "comfort," "convenience," "revenue," and "profit"; these are all now obsolete or rare.

The meanings of the term that concern us most both emerge in the fifteenth century. Here are the *Oxford English Dictionary* entries:

3a. A natural resource, material, etc., which is of use or value to mankind; a useful product

3b. A thing produced for use or sale; a piece of merchandise; an article of commerce

These entries provide *distinct* definitions of "commodity." In the first we have a *natural* and *useful* thing; in the second we have a *produced* and *exchangeable* thing.

Our work on historical social orders and modes of production in Part I should have equipped us with a set of lenses through which to parse these definitions. That is, given the work we have done before, we should see that 3a offers a broad, general, and *transhistorical* meaning for "commodity." In the sense of 3a, in the sense of useful natural resources, we can surely find "commodities" at all places and times in history. But 3b is different: as a thing **produced for sale**, we really only find this type of "commodity," in a strict sense, where we also find a capitalist mode of production. After all, in defining the commodity, 3b repeats many elements of our own definition of a capitalist mode of production. Under feudal or tributary modes of production, goods were not produced with the explicit intention to sell them; this practice occurs only within a capitalist social order. We can draw a preliminary conclusion by saying that 3b gives the definition of a **capitalist commodity**, while 3a provides a much more generic definition of a useful **good**, one not at all peculiar to capitalism.

Since our task in this part of the book is to focus on key elements within a capitalist social order—that is, we assume throughout that our analysis applies only to capitalist economics—3b gives us a perfectly functional, viable starting point for trying to conceptualize and analyze commodities. In addition, however, we must be very clear about *why* definition 3a proves unhelpful for our purposes. Since we want to know specifically about capitalist commodities, we need to maintain the analytic distinction between a generic idea of a "useful good" and the specific notion of an "exchangeable good produced for sale." From here on out, then, whenever we refer to commodities, we do so in the narrower sense of 3b; that is, we always mean *capitalist commodities*, even if we will often just write "commodities."

And this brings us back to Robinsonades and the lack of definitions in current textbooks. If the *OED* proves so helpful, why don't current economics textbooks offer a short definition of commodities as "goods produced for sale"? One answer may be because modern economics, and the neoclassical paradigm of economics as a whole, *does not want to distinguish between 3a and 3b*. Instead, they aim to subtly combine the two definitions, to conflate them as if they were the same. This is precisely what a state-of-nature story achieves: it **naturalizes commodities.**[2] And if something is "natural," then it is also *obvious*, such that no definition would be required. In the state of nature, everything is a commodity, so there's no need either to define a commodity or to distinguish it from any other good or resource. If everything is a commodity then nothing is a commodity in a way that makes a difference.

What a Commodity Is *Not*

Our task here is the opposite of the Robinsonade: not to naturalize commodities, but to *denaturalize* them, to bring them into a clear light such that we can observe the specific role they play within a capitalist mode of production. Rather than *conflate* definitions 3a and 3b, we will vigilantly maintain the gap between those two definitions. Everything hinges on holding on to the difference between 3a and 3b, because only if we can preserve an analytic separation between these two will we be able to grasp the deeper meaning and importance of commodities, and only then can we rigorously understand their role in capitalism.

One way to achieve this is simply by listing some examples of goods that may at first glance appear to be commodities according to definition 3a, but in terms of our analysis are *not* commodities according to 3b (i.e., they are not *capitalist commodities*).[3] We will therefore treat them as *not* commodities at all, distinguishing proper commodities in the capitalist sense from other goods, resources, or useful things. Let's map out a few cases.

If you go on a hike where the trail passes a ridgeline with a group of blackberry bushes full of ripe blackberries, and you decide to pick and eat a few to sustain yourself for the coming miles, **those blackberries are not commodities.** They are obviously natural resources or natural goods, and given the specifics of this case, they are even more obviously *useful objects*. But they are not commodities; they were neither produced for exchange nor exchanged. We might complicate this case by asking whether it matters if we find the blackberries on public land (in a national forest) or on private land (along the fence line of a private residence). The answer: it might matter for legal property relations, as it's possible that you have stolen private property if you picked the blackberries from a bush on land not owned by you, but it matters not at all for the definition of a commodity since, regardless of who owns the land (and whether any property laws were violated), the blackberries remain useful goods appropriated for personal use, not produced commodities manufactured for market sale.

We can then shift to a second case where, rather than picking blackberries we found in the wild, we instead decide to grow tomatoes in our backyard. This practice involves much more planning and time, as we need to buy and plant in the spring, cultivate and care for the plants during the summer, and harvest in the fall. Our enjoyment of these tomatoes—when we eat them on our BLT sandwiches in August and September—therefore far exceeds the temporary respite the blackberries gave us on our hike. Our relationship to the tomatoes therefore proves very different (perhaps much more meaningful to us) than our relationship to the blackberries. But one thing remains the same: like the blackberries, **these tomatoes are not commodities.**

We might want to say that the tomatoes are "produced" in the sense that we spent some money and lots of time and labor growing them (and thus, in a sense, *making* them). But they are not produced for exchange, for sale, for profit. They were never part of a capitalist production process, and therefore they are not capitalist commodities. Here we see that "production" in the sense of a capitalist social order's *mode of production* cannot be reduced to "activity" or "labor" or "work" but rather must be connected to a broader *system of production for exchange.* The productive process must be organized and planned in relation to market exchange. Thus we can see that with respect to production, the difference between the blackberry case and the tomato case is one of quality or intensity, not one of kind. We had to expend energy and time to pick the blackberries; the important point with the tomatoes is not the difference (more time) but the similarity—all the productive energies were devoted to obtaining the natural good for our own *use* (not for exchange).

Now let's add a wrinkle to the tomato case. What if our harvest of tomatoes proves so bountiful that we simply have too many tomatoes to eat before they go bad? We can do what many home tomato growers do: give bags and bags of tomatoes to all our friends and neighbors. But *giving* is not the same as market *exchange*; no money or profit is involved, and thus the mere fact that our friends receive and consume our tomatoes does not change the basic structure. The tomatoes are *still* **not commodities.**

How about (second wrinkle) if instead of giving them away, we took some of our tomatoes to the local farmer's market and sold them? This case proves to be the most subtle, and therefore *the most important for our entire effort to specify the definition of a commodity.* It seems simple to conclude that here, in this case, we finally have a commodity: a produced good sold on the market. And in one sense, that's true enough, but now we must recall and emphasize a crucial point from Part I: markets and market exchange prove ubiquitous in history, yet neither the existence of markets nor even the capitalist use of markets is enough to produce capitalism (i.e., a capitalist social order). As we discussed, some goods were sold at markets for money under feudalism. More significantly, some actors used those markets for capitalist purposes (coming to the market with money and then using it to make more money). But capitalism is more than the capitalist use of markets; it is the reorganization of production for market exchange.

So what can we say about the extra tomatoes that we sold at the farmer's market? These tomatoes were both produced and exchanged, but **they were not produced *in order* to be exchanged**. The most precise formulation of this case is to say that here *we have a capitalist use of goods that are not technically commodities*; we treated the tomatoes *as if* they were capitalist commodities.[4] However, in the strict, technical sense, **the tomatoes are still not capitalist commodities** because they were not produced within an overall system of production designed for the goal of realizing profit through market exchange.[5] We should note that our tomato sellers are certainly not going to make an actual "profit" in any case; they are simply recouping some of the money (and time) they spent on growing tomatoes for noncapitalist uses—that is, for their own consumption (in eating) and enjoyment (in growing).

This brings us to a final case: here we organize and carry out a hike to find and pick blueberries, place them in bags, bring them home, box them up, and then take them to the farmer's market on Saturday to sell. There's not much else to say, *these* **blueberries are commodities**: they were produced for market exchange.[6] (And the blueberries we picked on private land *would* have been commodities had that land been a commercial blueberry farm; this would then be an example of theft of commodities.) Both this case and that of the extra tomatoes sold at market raise an important but separate question of whether or not our sale generates any *profit*. We will analyze this question in detail in the next chapter, but here we conclude that only in this last case, the case of the blueberries, do we meet the criteria for our technical definition of a capitalist commodity.

The Nature of the Commodity

Given this precise *definition* of the commodity, how do we understand what a commodity *is*? How do we analyze the role or function it plays in capitalist economics? Once we grasp the fact that the commodity is not *merely or simply* a useful good, we can begin to see that *the commodity is unique in its nature and uniquely important to capitalist social orders.* The commodity is unique because it has a dual nature. In philosophical language we can say that the commodity is metaphysically twofold; in its nature it is two, not one. In plainer language, a commodity is always two things at once. When we place the commodity under the microscope, we see its two-ness.[7]

First, a commodity is indeed "a useful product" (in the language of definition 3a); a commodity is useful, it satisfies human needs. To express this first aspect of the commodity, we will say that a commodity is a use-value. Moreover, each distinct commodity has a distinct use-value, so every commodity is a use-value, but different commodities are not the same use-values. The use-value of a hammer is nothing like the use-value of a cup of coffee. Both are commodities; hence both are use-values. But they are distinct and incommensurable use-values: if you need to pound in a nail, no amount of coffee will accomplish the task.[8] As use-values, all commodities are distinct.

Second, as a good produced for market exchange, a commodity turns out to be much more than a "useful product." Given its relation to the market, *a commodity is also a valuable good.* As we know, any commodity can be swapped for other commodities as equivalents, $C \rightarrow C$. This exchange relation conveys the second aspect of the commodity's existence: a commodity is an exchange-value. Whether we express this exchange-value in monetary terms, *as price,* or merely in the proportional terms of basic exchange, we can see that the commodity has a second existence beyond use-value—this is its existence as exchange-value.

We must highlight a crucial fact here: the twofold metaphysical existence of capitalist commodities is not a physical property of those commodities, and it is not given to them by nature. The dual nature of commodities comes about because they are products of a capitalist mode of production; it is a result of the fact that they are produced for profitable market exchange. We can clarify this essential point by returning to our earlier cases: the backyard tomato and the ridge-line blackberries do not have a twofold existence—they are only useful items. Only a good or service produced within a capitalist mode of production becomes doubled as use-value and exchange-value. The

What Is Bitcoin?

Bitcoin is a digital "coin" created and transferred on a peer-to-peer cryptographically secured computer network, and by far the most famous example of a "cryptocurrency"—defined as a digital asset that serves as a medium of exchange. In other words, bitcoin purports to be money (because it performs money functions) and evangelists for bitcoin often suggest it has the capacity to replace national currencies, providing a more secure and efficient monetary system: less prone to corruption or political manipulation and protected from inflation by the fixed, limited supply of digital coins. In recent years there has been much debate over the basic question "is bitcoin money?" that has proceeded alongside the sharp rise in the price of bitcoin (as measured in national currencies). It may seem odd to address bitcoin here, and not in the previous chapter on money, but there are very good reasons for this approach.

First, Chapter 4 provided a clear litmus test for money. Money is credit/debt. For something to be money it must appear *both* as an asset on the balance sheet of the person/institution that holds the credit *and* as a liability on the balance sheet of the person/institution that holds the debt. Bitcoin completely fails this test. The bitcoin network verifies ownership of positive assets: it is more like a property registry that verifies title to assets than it is like a money ledger that registers both credits and corresponding liabilities. To hold a bitcoin is not to hold a credit against a debtor, but merely to claim ownership of a "digital coin." Bitcoin is not money.

Second, Chapter 5 has helped to illuminate the complex nature of the commodity, and this will help us to move beyond the "is it money?" question to a deeper one: What is bitcoin? As the title to the original bitcoin white paper by "Satoshi Nakamoto" makes clear, the bitcoin technology is explicitly designed to create "digital cash," an asset that does not depend on "third parties." In other words, the aim of bitcoin is to use blockchain technology to mimic the construction of a commodity of intrinsic value that can circulate as a form of commodity money. Bitcoin is digital gold. We can now see that unlike real gold, unlike any real commodity, bitcoin is only an exchange-value. Bitcoin is not a commodity because it is not twofold; it is not a use-value. Therefore bitcoin is a faux commodity.

"nature" of the twofold commodity is not purely "natural": it depends on the social order in which it is produced. This is a *social* nature, which makes it contingent on the social function of commodities within a capitalist social order.

Produced goods become exchange-values only when they are made for markets—that is, only under capitalism. If there were no markets at all, then there would be no exchange-values. Further, if we produced almost exclusively for non-market purposes (as, for example, under feudalism), the objects we produced would have a single existence as useful goods. But if we produce primarily for market exchange, then this very social, political, and cultural system of production entails that the objects we produce are dual: use-values and exchange-values.

The Impossible Equation: $xA = yB$

The commodity's existence as exchange-value proves no less real than its existence as use-value, but its **exchange-value is a** *social existence*. That is, the commodity continues to exist as use-value even after I purchase it (for consumption) and remove it from the market. If I buy an heirloom tomato from the farmers' market, bring it home, and prepare to eat it, it still serves a use to me that is not dependent on the market or the larger social order. Unless and until it rots, I can always eat the tomato and satisfy my hunger. But the tomato's existence as exchange-value proves totally different. If I am in the business of growing heirloom tomatoes for sale at the farmers' market, then the tomato's existence *as exchange-value* proves contingent and variable in a way utterly unlike its existence as use-value. This is because **as exchange-value the commodity's existence is always social, always relational.** Let's explore this point in more depth.

The cup of coffee is a use-value when it provides me with a flavorful warm dose of morning caffeine. But when I consider the cup of coffee in relation to some other commodity, it exists utterly differently; it becomes an exchange-value. If I take my cup of coffee and a book and try to compare them, I quickly find that *as use-values* they are incomparable. They satisfy radically distinct uses. If I want to read a great fiction story, the coffee is of no use to me whatsoever; if I want to wake myself up for an afternoon of answering emails, the book is similarly useless. But as exchange-values, the two are readily comparable, because we can easily see that the book would exchange with the coffee at a rough ratio of four-to-one. In other words, the market price of the coffee is about $2.50, while the market price of the book is $9.99; as exchange-values, the book and the coffee are both values (expressible in money terms) and are thus not only comparable but ultimately *equivalent* (assuming we get the ratios correct). As exchange-values, commodities are nothing more or less than equivalent relations to other commodities. The value of my coffee is one-fourth of a book; or expressed in a formula, we can say that four coffees = one book.

We need to pause here to observe and to consider the truly odd nature of this formula. The algebraic equal sign $(=)$ makes it seem as if we merely have two entities that are the same. But books and coffee are not the same. Moreover, the relation of commodities under capitalism is not reducible to algebra, and that is because **the coffee and the books are both equal and unequal, both the same, and utterly distinct.** The formula "four coffees are worth one book" is not just an equation or a proportional relation between two exchange-values; the formula conveys the fundamental value expression within capitalist exchange. In this formula we express the "value" of the coffee by linking it to the material object of the book. That is, the use-value of the book serves to express the exchange-value of the coffee. But the formula can never alter the use-values of the two goods, and the use-value of coffee and books can never be "equal." Therefore the formula "four coffees are worth one book" expresses both an identity and an antagonism (nonidentity).

This analysis raises a central question: How can two utterly distinct and incommensurable use-values—two different material objects with different uses—be rendered *equal* to one another in the first place? What does it mean to say that coffee = book? That seems like an impossible equation. Here we come to a deeper and richer understanding of a capitalist social order. **Capitalism is that system which makes such an impossible equation possible.** Outside of a capitalist social formation books and coffee and hammers are all different things. But under capitalism they remain different and yet also become the same. All capitalist commodities are twofold; they are use-values and exchange-values. As such, the physical body of one such commodity can be used to express the exchange-value of another. They all take on the form of value: they all become exchange-values, and as such—that is, as values—they can be equated with one another.

This deduction leads to two crucial follow-ups. First, a clarification: even though a capitalist social order makes a certain impossible equation between commodities possible, this does not undo our earlier and still fundamental analysis about the nature of the commodity: because commodities remain twofold in their very nature, they are never all "the same." Though they be equated with one another as exchange-values, commodities remain distinct as use-values. Here we should emphasize that even though under market exchange we often privilege exchange-values (money seems to be all that matters), use-values remain essential. A commodity without use is no commodity at all. The commodity's existence as exchange-value depends on its existence as use-value since a commodity that has no use at all cannot be sold.

Second, this raises an indispensable question that remains for us to answer in the coming chapters: *How* does a capitalist order effect this result? How does the circulation of commodities in capitalist production and exchange impose this **form of value** (exchange-value, money value) on all produced goods and services? The beginnings of an answer can be found in the secret of *profit*.

Notes

1. As we noted in Chapter 3, noncapitalist social orders may also produce goods that are later exchanged on the market, sometimes even for profit. But a capitalist social order has a *capitalist mode of production*, which means that market exchange forms the fundamental basis of societal production.

2. We have now found ourselves repeatedly contextualizing or historicizing that which neoclassical economics seeks to naturalize, and at this stage a reader might wonder *why* this tendency to naturalize seems so common in modern economics. Of numerous possible answers, one stands out: if the building blocks of economics are natural (literally found in nature) then they are universal in the sense of transhistorical, and this means that the

principles of modern economics would be true for all times and places. It would make economics a general science, just like physics. Part I of this book was devoted to an alternative approach that situates economics *in* history. As we focus our analysis in Part II on some of the fundamental elements of capitalist economics (money, commodities, profit) we repeatedly find that our analysis differs dramatically from that of the neoclassical paradigm.

3. Our more rigorous and technical definition of a capitalist commodity will also allow us to clarify the relationship between physical (material) goods, on the one hand, and services, on the other. A "commodity" in the sense of a thing produced for exchange can be *either* an object *or* a service. **Services are commodities too.** As Michael Heinrich has helpfully explained, the difference between the two consists mainly in the fact that an object is produced before it is sold, whereas a service is often sold (even if it is not fully paid for) *before it is produced.* The shoemaker produces the shoes first and *then* offers them for sale. In contrast, the Uber driver makes the offer *first*, and only after the exchange has occurred—i.e., when I agree to pay by clicking in the app—does the driver then *produce* the commodity by providing the service, by driving me from place A to place B. In this example, the particular commodity sold is nothing more or less than that service provided; or, to state it the other way around, the service here is a commodity. It is worth noting that while the materiality of a service is often different from a typical good (because the service is not a singular concrete object that I can hold in my hands), this does not mean that services are "immaterial." The Uber driver has to obtain a car, a license, and gasoline, and then has to expend fuel (and rubber and oil) as she moves me through the physical space of the world from place to place. Services are material activities and practices, as anyone who has ever worked in the "service industry" surely knows.

4. It proves absolutely crucial to note that capitalist social orders **routinely treat noncommodities like commodities.** Therefore, even if an object does not meet the strict criteria for our definition of a capitalist commodity, that object (from tomatoes to bitcoins) still may be bought and sold, speculated upon, and thus used to make money, just like a commodity. Within a capitalist mode of production the capitalist use of the market expands dramatically, to such an extent that large numbers of entities can be bought and sold. Nonetheless, the mere fact that something is bought and sold does not change it into a commodity, yet a capitalist mode of production depends on the (continued) existence of commodities.

5. This example differs subtly but significantly from cases where one *resells* goods that were already capitalist commodities to begin with. Think about

the example of eBay sellers. Some people use eBay as a business, selling goods they've acquired there or elsewhere in order to make money; others just use eBay to get rid of old items they no longer have a use for. If I am in the latter category and I sell my old iPhone on eBay, I seem to be doing something very similar to the person who sold their extra homegrown tomatoes at market, but the difference is that *the iPhone was already a commodity*. I am merely *reselling* it. The business eBay users are also usually resellers, but they are more like early merchant capitalists who use the market to make money, though they are not producers. Finally, some eBay and Etsy sellers are, in fact, producers, and in this case they are clearly selling commodities (goods they have produced with the explicit intention of selling for profit.)

6. Notice that capitalist "production" does not have to involve factory systems or robots or large teams of workers. Any expenditure of energy, time, work, or money to obtain or make an object counts as production. The key for all of our examples lies not in the different types or intensities of production but in the relation of production to market exchange.

7. Not literally! "Microscope" is a metaphor for our own conceptual analysis.

8. Some commodities, of course, have overlapping domains of use, so Pepsi and Coke can both be used to satisfy a desire for a sugary cola beverage. This does not change the fact that each use-value is distinct from all the others; we know that no one who truly wants a Coke will purchase Pepsi when Coke is available. Pepsi is of *limited* use-value for the Coke drinker, while a hammer is of no use at all.

6

Profit

Just as commodities had already been at the core of all of our discussions of capitalist economics, so profit has always been the *target*. Profit first appeared in this book when we introduced the code for capitalist production, $M \rightarrow C...P...C' \rightarrow M'$. **Profit is the goal**; it is the intention, the aim, the very purpose of capitalist economic motion. The system cannot be initiated without putting a sum of money to use with the express goal of turning it into a greater sum of money, and the system cannot be effectively realized without producing that result. Profit is the "prime" symbol in the final term of the capitalist code, M'. In one sense, then, we have already defined profit on the basis of the existence of ΔM.

But we have not fully answered arguably the most important question in the history of economic thought: *What is profit?* Despite our emphasis here on the apparent (and central) significance of the question, we must highlight the fact that the vast majority of economic writings do not even broach this question, much less provide an adequate answer. The wager of this chapter is that our development of a broader and deeper understanding of both the capitalist mode of production and the primary elements that constitute capitalist relations (money and commodities) will give us the tools required to uncover a more rigorous and more sophisticated understanding of the nature and structure of capitalist profit.

The Answer Is Not on the Spreadsheet

Unlike the key terms from the two previous chapters (money and commodities), which largely went overlooked or submerged in standard economics textbooks but were never clearly defined or conceptualized, nothing could be easier for the neoclassical paradigm of economics

Capitalist Economics. Samuel A. Chambers, Oxford University Press. © Oxford University Press 2022.
DOI: 10.1093/oso/9780197556887.003.0007

than to define profit. Every textbook will say that *profit = revenue minus cost*. If you want to find profit, simply do the books for the capitalist enterprise: add up all the costs to produce commodities in one column; add up the sales totals and all other income generators in a second column; and subtract the first column total from the second. The final result is "net revenue," which is simply another name for profit. According to mainstream economics and all business school teachings, profit is nothing more or less than this spreadsheet result.

In one sense, of course, this is perfectly true. If you are a small business owner, all that matters is net revenue: Are you making enough money each month to both keep the business open and pay your own personal bills? But this is not a rigorous analysis. The economics textbook definition of profit is embarrassingly inadequate. To see why, just imagine if a physics textbook explained the properties of H_2O and the transformation of a liquid into a gas by saying this: if you place water in a kettle and put it on the stove, boiling occurs when steam comes out the top of the kettle. That's valid as an empirical description. But it doesn't explain anything; it doesn't help us understand the nature of water or the process by which heated liquids transform into gases.

Profit as net revenue has a comparable empirical validity, yet it similarly fails to explain anything. Knowing that enterprises that remain in business generate revenues in excess of costs does not tell us anything about the nature of profit in a capitalist system; it doesn't shed any light on how profit is possible in the first place, on where it comes from, or on what it means for an entire social order to revolve around, to be organized according to, this principle.

Searching for ΔM

The definition of profit as net revenue is itself a reflection of a piece of our capitalist code, and this insight might provide an entry point for our effort to conceptualize profit more rigorously. In the capitalist mode of production, profit is the goal. The end point of the process is M', which we previously defined as follows:

$$M' = M + \Delta M$$

Notice what happens if we rearrange terms; we can produce a formula that *looks like* the definition of net revenue:

$$\Delta M = M' - M$$

ΔM takes the place of net revenue; M' takes the place of gross revenue; and M takes the place of costs. But also notice what has changed in this translation into our capitalist code. "Net revenue" is strictly a *calculated result*; it is the output of a basic accounting formula of addition and subtraction on the spreadsheet. Put differently, "net revenue" is never directly observed—and certainly never grasped conceptually. Instead, "sales" and "costs" are measured directly, empirically, and net revenue is then produced as a mathematical result. Net revenue is what's left over, the output of a spreadsheet formula.

ΔM proves to be something quite different. As a symbol in our capitalist code, ΔM is not directly observable (or measurable). However, ΔM is a concept designed to help us grasp the structure and process of capitalist production and exchange. As a conceptual category, ΔM makes it possible to raise the essential question: *What is profit?* ΔM **is not profit, but the existence of profit depends fundamentally on the existence of ΔM**. In order for it to be possible to start with M and arrive at M', somehow a ΔM must come into being during capitalist production. To pursue the question of profit means to search for this emergence of ΔM.

Surplus

ΔM is the most concise and precise symbolic expression of what we today call capitalist *growth*, but growth is just another name for surplus. We previously encountered the concept of surplus when describing a feudal social order in which serfs work the land of the lord, producing not only enough food to feed themselves and their families but also a *surplus* that the lord uses to feed himself and his family. Under feudalism, this surplus was directly visible: the serf literally *grew extra food* for the lord. Now, with the concept of ΔM, we have encountered a capitalist concept of surplus. In this case we have a surplus of money—that is, *surplus value*. A period of capitalist production starts with a quantum of value (a certain amount of money) and ends with an increased or augmented quantum of value (a larger sum of money). ΔM expresses this increase, this growth, this surplus of value.[1]

We must carefully and consistently distinguish this idea of *total surplus* (and surplus value) from the idea of *gains in a zero-sum game*. For example, say that eight friends meet for an evening to play poker. Each player buys in (exchanges money for chips) for $100, the group gambles for a number of hours, and at the end of the night everyone cashes out (exchanges chips for money). Assume at the end of the evening that the cash-outs look like this: $200, $150, $150, $100, $80, $50, $50, $20. Three players won, one broke even, and four players lost. The three winners took home net winnings of $100, $50, and $50, respectively. Those winnings are not surplus.

The idea of true surplus, of overall growth, proves utterly distinct. To get to the notion of *surplus* (which ΔM represents) we would need to have a poker game that worked on a totally different basis. The buy-ins would be the same as our first example, but the payouts would look like this: $275, $225, $200, $100, $80, $50, $50, $20. Crucially, the surplus here is still not the winnings that the top players take home, neither individually ($175, $125, $100) nor collectively ($400). The surplus is the difference between the total amount of buy-ins ($800) and the total amount of payouts ($1,000). ΔM is this $200; it is the total surplus produced by the poker game as a whole. (Notice that this $200 only shows up in the overall totals and not in any individual take-home amounts—a point we will return to.)

"Winnings" in a zero-sum game cannot and do not serve as the basis of a capitalist social order. If we want to understand ΔM (the secret to profit) we will not find it merely by looking at the winning players; we have to look at the system overall and figure out how it generates an absolute surplus. Our imaginary poker game provides a powerful heuristic precisely because it is made up: no one has ever heard of a poker game that pays out more than the buy-ins. But this is precisely the idea of a capitalist mode of production: it is a system that is meant to produce a true surplus, an absolute augmentation, such that it generates more value than it starts with.

A capitalist social order only comes into being on the basis of this type of authentic surplus. As we analyzed in some detail in Part I, merely using a market for exchange to swindle someone else will not result in a cumulative system of capitalism. So although the market can be used for capitalist purposes, that use of the market does not in and of itself result in capitalism. Using a market for capitalist purposes is a lot like our first poker game: it might lead to winnings for some people, but it remains zero-sum. It does not spark unique economic creation, fundamental augmentation, or what we normally call "growth."[2]

This explains why our definition of capitalism—that is, of a capitalist social order—rests on the existence of a capitalist mode of *production*. Production proves primary because only through capitalist production can we derive a capitalist system based on the *generation of surplus*. In Part I we described how capitalism is never a matter of exchange only, but rather a relation between exchange and production, between the capitalist use of markets and the rearrangement of the production process toward the ultimate end of selling commodities for profit. We can now see another reason why this account holds: the capitalist use of markets only leads to a degenerate form of M', because on its own (in the absence of a capitalist mode of production) it only leads to "winnings."

To find ΔM we have to track down surplus (and surplus value), and only then can we explain profit.

The Secret to Surplus Value

The key to surplus value can only be found within the terms of a capitalist mode of production, which we now (after the last two chapters) understand as a process dependent on the circulation of money and commodities. Hence the secret to surplus value lies in the very nature of money and commodities. Let's start to unpack these claims by returning to the unique and peculiar existence of the capitalist commodity.

Chapter 5 delineated the complex relationship between use-value and exchange-value. We can now build on that conceptualization of the commodity in its twofold nature to enumerate the required conditions for the creation of surplus. The generation of surplus value depends on the possibility that there exists a commodity such that when we *use it* (i.e., consume it), that use itself produces a quantum of value greater than the market exchange-value of the commodity itself. In other words, the key to profit lies in the following code: $U_c \rightarrow V > EV_c$. This formula states that the quantity of value generated by the use of the commodity is greater than the market exchange-value of the same commodity. Surplus value is therefore the difference between the commodity's exchange-value and the value it generates in use: $SV = V - EV_c$, where V is a function of U_c.

Notice the strangeness of this formula, as well as how difficult it will be to find a commodity that meets the needed criteria. To see this, imagine a standard commodity—let's call it the *profit commodity*, C_p — one that everyone could purchase on Amazon for a reasonable price and that satisfied these specified conditions. Let's assume that C_p is some piece of computer technology, such that when you *run* it, it directly generates value (i.e., money). To simplify, we can also assume that the device can only run for a fixed amount of time, at the end of which it cannot run any longer (perhaps its software crashes and becomes permanently corrupted, perhaps its nonreplaceable and non-renewable energy source depletes, or perhaps it literally self-destructs). To continue specifying terms that meet our requirements, let's assume that the C_p runs for 4 hours and generates \$50 of value, and further that the market price of the C_p is \$40. These values would plug nicely into our formula to generate our expected profit: $\$40 \rightarrow C_p...U_c...\$50$. First we purchase the profit commodity, then we use it, and in the end we have more money than we started with. Notice here that the "use" of the commodity takes the place of both the production process (...P...) and the sale of the finished commodity (C') in our general formula for capitalist production, $M \rightarrow C...P...C' \rightarrow M'$.

In abstract terms, this works. But we should immediately see a big problem with it—namely, if the *use* of this commodity (U_c) produces more value than the commodity's price, then wouldn't literally everyone in the world (at least everyone who had or who could borrow

$40) want to buy that commodity? And if so, wouldn't this drive the price up? Indeed, we know not only that the price of the profit commodity would rise, but also that the price would rise all the way to the level of the value that its use generates (i.e., $50). Because even if the price of C_p was $49.99, then one could still generate limitless profits merely by buying unlimited amounts of C_p. However, as we have shown, the fact that the use of C_p generates $50 means that the price of C_p will be no lower than $50. And now we are out of luck—because if the price of C_p is $50, then it no longer meets the specified criteria for the profit commodity.

Our example can in fact be used to demonstrate the pricing of *raw materials*. You will recall from Chapter 4 that "raw materials" are commodities used in the production process. These are the first C in the general code for capitalist production: the commodities we purchase as inputs to the production process (the result of which is C'). What do such commodities cost? The same amount as the value they contribute to the finished good (the commodity for sale). If I use 100 pounds of cotton in my production of cloth, and the cotton contributes $75 to the total value of the finished cloth, then we can deduce that the fair market price of cotton (around which it will surely fluctuate) is about $0.75 per pound. If it were possible for me to buy cotton at $0.50 per pound, then that would mean I could spend $50 on 100 pounds of cotton, and the cotton would contribute $75 to my finished product. Everyone already in the business of cloth production (and a few others besides) would therefore want to buy as much cotton as they could, thereby driving the price of cotton up . . . to $0.75 per pound. The market price of production commodities will remain in rough parity with the value that those commodities contribute to the finished goods.

Yet in explaining the pricing of production goods, we have failed entirely in our goal—namely, the effort to describe a "profit commodity." We started by assuming a market price for C_p of $40 and the generation of value (through C_p's use/consumption) of $50, but those two assumptions prove untenable. Either the commodity will not generate that much value when used, or its price will not remain that low; **it is impossible for a basic commodity to directly generate value greater than its own market price.** We can conclude that there is no such thing as a "profit commodity" strictly in the realm of exchange—that is, one we could buy on the market, consume directly, and thereby generate surplus value.

Back to Production (and the Search for ΔC)

We carried out our (failed) attempt to meet the criteria for surplus value through the construction of a "profit commodity" by remaining in the realm of exchange. We might suspect that the problem with our reasoning lies there. Earlier we substituted the commodity's *use* (...*U*...) for a production process (...*P*...). But the two processes are not the same; we cannot substitute one for the other. The production process does not merely *use* a commodity; it *transforms* one commodity into an utterly new, entirely different commodity ($C...P...C'$). If we consider the case more carefully, we realize that it makes no sense to assume that the consumption of a commodity would generate value directly, in the form of money. There are two types of consumption. *End consumption* (or personal consumption) happens at the conclusion of the economic process; through this type of consumption the commodity is destroyed (or gradually used up over time) to satisfy individual wants or needs (eating food, wearing clothes, living in our house or apartment). *Productive consumption* occurs in the middle of, and as a central element in, the capitalist mode of production; it involves the destruction of one commodity (C) in order to produce a new one (C'). This means that a certain, special type of consumption lies at the center of the production process (...*P*...). In fact, if we look at the overall code for the capitalist mode of production we can observe that "productive consumption" has an implicit role to play as part of P, while end consumption lies after the production process, after exchange, and therefore in a way *outside of* the economic system.

This clarification of productive consumption allows us to underscore the point that surplus cannot be generated through end consumption, which means the key to surplus cannot be found in exchange alone. This leads us to the following crucial, if still interim, conclusion: if we are going to locate the process of profit generation, we must look for it in production.

This provides a good opportunity for twisting together a number of threads in the book. Let's start by returning to the code for the capitalist use of markets: $M \rightarrow C \rightarrow M'$. We know this code reduces to the essential idea that at the core of capitalism lies the use of money to generate more money, $M \rightarrow M'$. We also know that $M' = M + \Delta M$ and that profit depends on (is not possible without) ΔM. Moreover, we can now bring into starker view a crucially important point that was only implicit earlier: ΔM **depends on an invisible** ΔC. That is, $C' = C + \Delta C$. ΔM *is only the realization of a change in value that was already present in* C', the finished good that is then sold at a profit.

This tells us that our search for the profit commodity was always in vain because the use of a commodity cannot directly generate value. Profit can only exist at the end of the process, as ΔM, if it somehow gets generated in the middle of the process, as ΔC. The realization of ΔM entails the prior existence of ΔC. Our search for ΔM—and with it our efforts to find the source and nature of profit—requires us to search for the source of ΔC.

This *change* in C that comes about during the production process cannot be inherent in the original C. Put differently, C does not become C' of its own volition, or as a part of its nature as a commodity; if it did, then it would always already be C'. Something must occur during the production process itself that gives us a commodity (C') that is worth more in value than the sum of the commodities (C) used to make it.[3]

Labor

Up to this point our analysis has left out one key element: the *content* of the production process. Production is not exchange; it is not the shuffling around of commodities, but rather the *creation* of new commodities out of old commodities. It is an active and transformative process; in production energy is expended in the form of *work*. ΔC emerges only as a result of this transformative energy process, as a result of work, of labor. As we will see in Chapter 8, the enterprise owner or entrepreneur plans and manages the production process, but beyond his organizational and executive activities, production always involves something more: the activity of humans and machines to transform raw materials into finished commodities.

To express this in our developing symbolic language, we can break down C into its constituent components: $C = MP + LP$. Prior to and in order to initiate the production process, the enterprise owner (the capitalist) must first purchase the "means of production" (MP) and "labor-power" (LP). "Means of production" merely expands upon the idea of "raw materials" (goods used for production) that we have already discussed. MP includes both raw materials (like cotton) that are completely used up, and tools and machinery (like sewing machines) that wear out over time. Our analysis has already shown that raw materials cannot function as "profit commodities" because their exchange-value will always end up roughly equal to the value they contribute to the finished good. The same logical argument applies to machine technology since any machine that produced "extra value" over and above its market price would immediately have its market price bid up as enterprise owners rushed to buy such a machine.

This brings us to labor. The first thing we need to say about labor is that in its general nature it is not capitalist. While labor is an essential and indispensable part of the capitalist production process, because every mode of production has labor at its core (the capitalist mode proving no exception), there is nothing about labor in general that makes it specifically "capitalist." Moreover, the criteria we established in Chapter 5 for specifying a *capitalist commodity* can be used to prove definitively that **labor is not a commodity**. Both the capacity for human labor and the active process of laboring (the practice) are not produced in order to be sold on the market. Labor is indelibly tied to human beings themselves, and human beings are not commodities; today, the law establishes that they cannot be bought and sold.[4]

This means that labor can never be a commodity in the same sense as the blueberries that we picked specifically to sell; at most, labor would be like the extra homegrown tomatoes that we decided to take to market only after the fact. Labor is not "produced" in order to sell. Therefore, if we are going to try to make sense of the practice of buying and selling "labor," we must start with the assertion that labor is, in fact, not a commodity; rather, labor is a member of a rather large set of entities that, under capitalism, we treat *like* commodities—even though they technically are *not* commodities. More importantly, labor is a special and distinguished member of that set. There are many items that are easy to treat as commodities. We may know that our homegrown tomatoes are not commodities because we produced them out of love and for the joy they gave us, not to bring them to market and sell to strangers. But the strangers at market who buy them do not care about any of this: our tomatoes look just like the heirloom tomatoes grown by the local farmer—the production differences disappear once both tomatoes show up at market with a price tag. **But labor does not work this way. We cannot separate our labor from our physical bodies. There is no simple way to treat labor like a commodity, to bring labor to market and sell it.**

Labor-Power

This produces a conundrum for capitalist production. The enterprise owner uses money to buy all the necessary components for initiating a production process, and labor is most definitely an essential component. **The capitalist needs to purchase labor, yet labor is not directly purchasable.** It is not a commodity in general, and it cannot be easily treated like a commodity because it is inalienable. Historically capitalist social orders came up with an ingenious solution to this problem: "wage work," or "contract labor." The enterprise owner "hires" the laborer to work for wages; that is, the two parties enter a mutual *contract* (whether formally or informally) where the capitalist agrees to pay wages and the worker agrees to labor for the capitalist. This wage contract makes it possible for the enterprise owner to pay for labor—in what appears to be a regular act of market exchange.

To our twenty-first-century ears this may sound utterly boring and banal, and not at all "ingenious"; obviously workers work for wages, what's the big deal about that? But we now have the tools to analyze this apparently obvious market transaction in much more careful detail. We can ask what *is* the big deal here, in the sense of trying to figure out what is really going on. The worker has not sold themself into slavery; indeed, the wage contract is meant to respect the autonomy and freedom of the worker to choose to work or not to work. Yet this also means that *labor itself has not been sold* since the worker's capacity to labor still belongs to him. What, then, actually occurs when I sign on to work at McDonald's for $10/hour?

The contract is the key. **The wage contract imposes the *form* of capitalist exchange on the relation between the worker and the capitalist**. That is, through the contract, *it is as if the worker sold a commodity and the capitalist bought a commodity*. In formal and legal terms, the wage contract is like any other property contract (e.g., the contract to buy/sell a house); the wage contract makes it possible to treat labor like a commodity.[5]

The thing that is bought/sold in the wage contract is the very concept of labor as a commodity; we can call this labor-power. **Labor-power is the thing that workers sell when they agree to work for a wage and the thing that an enterprise owner buys when they hire workers. Labor-power is the unique capitalist commodity.**[6] Labor-power has no empirical referent; we cannot point to it concretely in the world (like we can the blueberries and the tomatoes and the Uber ride). It exists in and through the very form imposed by the wage contract. This doesn't make labor-power a fantasy or a falsehood; it is real because the wage contract does in fact create the conditions in which a worker can sell and the capitalist can buy "labor-power." Moreover, the concrete practices of laboring are no less material (work is still work) because of the unique nature of labor-power as a commodity.

To sum up: the wage contract makes possible a market exchange between worker and capitalist. What is sold in that exchange is not *labor* per se, because that proves physically and conceptually impossible. What is sold is the peculiar capitalist commodity "labor-power."

From Labor-Power to Surplus Value

If labor-power is a full-fledged capitalist commodity, then it should meet the commodity criteria. First, the exchange-value of labor-power is simple; it is what the capitalist pays and the worker receives through the wage contract; **the exchange-value of labor-power is the wage.** Next, we can remind ourselves that labor-power is a production commodity. The enterprise owner starts the production process by buying production commodities (C), and these are composed of two elements, means of production (MP) and labor-power (LP). Hence our formula, $C = MP + LP$. Thus, the use-value of labor-power is the utility of that commodity when implemented in the production process. In other words, the use-value of labor-power is the actual labor done by the worker—within the production process and according to the terms of the wage contract. If you are a capitalist who has bought labor-power from me, then you *use* that commodity by setting me to work in your system of production. In concrete terms, if the wage contract is for one week only, at 40 hours per week and $15/hour, then the exchange-value of labor-power is $600, and the use-value is 40 hours of labor.

Now let's plug these simple numbers into a slightly expanded example of a capitalist production process. Assume the single worker at $600/week is the only laborer hired by the capitalist; assume further that the production period for the finished commodity is one week, that the price of means of production is $400, and that the product sells for $1,100. This gives us:

$$M = \$1,000$$

$$LP = \$600$$

$$MP = \$400$$

$$C = MP + LP = \$1,000$$

$$C' = \$1,100$$

$$M' = \$1,100$$

The numbers here follow the basic rules of capitalist production, whereby C' must be greater than C, and they lead us to reiterate the basic question that has driven this entire chapter: Where does the extra $100, the ΔC, come from?

But with the introduction of the concept of labor-power, we now have the answer: labor-power fulfills the function that we assigned earlier to the "profit commodity" (C_p). We represented that function in formal terms as follows: if a commodity is the profit commodity, then the value its use produces will be greater than its exchange-value, $U_c \rightarrow V > EV_c$. **Labor-power is the profit commodity.** In our example, the capitalist paid $600 for labor-power, but after using that commodity (as the labor of the worker) in the production process, the finished good, C', contained $100 of extra value. We know that the ΔC of $100 cannot come from the purchased means of production, MP, since if it did, the market price of MP would be driven up. Therefore the only possible source of ΔC is LP. Labor-power is that unique capitalist commodity that when used in the production process creates more value than its own market exchange-value. The purchase and use of labor-power is the secret to capitalist surplus, which is *the source of all profit*.[7]

The "Labor Market"

For close readers, our climactic conclusion to the search for capitalist surplus should immediately register a critical response. Why is LP not subject to the same market constraints as MP? In every other case we rejected the claim to the title of "profit commodity" because any commodity whose use generated more value than its market price would immediately see that market price driven up until the gap $V > EV_c$ disappeared. Shouldn't the same thing happen with LP? If I can purchase labor-power on the open market for less than its use generates in my production process, won't other enterprise owners bid up the price of LP until the gap disappears?

We can outline two distinct but related answers. First, for every other commodity (for MP) the competitive market price simply is the amount of value that the production commodity contributes to the finished commodity. However, for every other commodity the capitalist is taking complete possession of the commodity and using it for production purposes, but with labor-power this is not the case. The labor-power that the capitalist "buys" remains directly connected to the physical body of the worker. This makes the "price" of labor-power (the wage) a unique and odd price: for every other commodity the market price will be governed not only by supply and demand but also by the costs of production. If the capitalist needs a widget for her production process and the market price is far higher than it would cost her to produce herself, she will simply produce the widget herself. And this basic market logic will tend to push down the price of the widget to something closer to its cost of production. This explanation raises an important question: What are the "costs of production" of labor-power? The complex answer requires seeing that the costs of production of labor-power are inseparable from the costs of "producing" the laborer herself. In other words, the driving force behind the cost of labor-power is the cost for a worker and her family to live. Furthermore, **there is almost always a gap between the cost of labor-power and the value the worker's labor contributes to a production process**. Hence we have now derived a second explanation for surplus value because we have again explained why the price of labor-power (wages) generally remains lower than the value that labor contributes to the product.

Second, the "market" for labor-power is unique. Put briefly, **there is no genuine (open and competitive) market for labor**, precisely for the reasons we detailed previously: labor is not an alienable and fungible commodity that can be bought and sold like any other. As we have just shown, labor always remains connected to, intimately bound up with, the body, mind, and soul of the laborer. The implications prove dramatic. The very idea of a market for exchange always depends on three figures: the buyer, the seller, and the commodity. The price of the commodity is therefore determined by the willingness of the buyers to buy and of the sellers to sell. Buyers can always choose *not* to buy; sellers can always choose *not* to sell. This latter point is crucial because it prevents prices from falling too low: if the price is too low, buyers can refuse to sell. But more than that, *producers can stop producing*, thereby decreasing supply in the future, which in turn raises prices.

But the market for labor-power is not really a market. In it, we only find two parties: capitalist buyers and worker sellers. Like all buyers, capitalists can choose not to buy if the price is too high. But the vast, vast majority of workers do not have that option: **workers must sell their labor-power**. Why? Because they live in a capitalist social order, and this means that they need *money* to acquire even the most basic and fundamental goods and services: food, shelter, clothing, transportation, education, and health care, just to name a few. Labor-power cannot be withheld from the market except through politics (e.g., a strike) because workers in general have no choice but to offer labor-power for sale for a wage; they need those wages in order to live.[8] Thus, in the narrow terms of basic economic forces and relations, labor-power is always available for sale, and this constant supply (and usually, with unemployment, excess supply) leads to lower prices. The lack of a fully realized market for labor leads, in turn, to a consistently lower price for labor-power, and this very fact makes it possible for labor-power to fulfill the role of the profit commodity.

We had previously posited capitalist social orders (through the definition of a capitalist mode of production) as unique in their capacity to produce surplus (M'). Other societies, with other modes of production, could contain "profits" in the limited sense of "net revenue," but these were only poker winnings (matched by losses on the other side) and never a true *surplus* that reflected a genuine growth or augmentation in the social order. The capitalist mode of production is marked by this deeper form of *surplus value*. We have now shown that such surplus cannot arise within exchange alone but depends, as capitalism itself does, on a unique relationship between production and exchange (production *for* exchange). The capitalist mode of production depends uniquely on "labor-power" as a commodity, and by reorganizing production around the market exchange and productive use of this commodity, the capitalist mode of production proves capable of generating surplus value—itself the key source for capitalist profit.

Notes

1. The French physiocrats, writing mainly in the eighteenth century, were the first to see this sort of surplus, in the form of *net product*. Their account seems almost childish from our perspective today, but it contains an essential insight into the capitalist mode of production. The physiocrats argued for the primacy of agricultural production because they saw in the nature of farming—planting seeds in the spring and harvesting crops in the autumn—the literal embodiment of *growth*, of augmentation, of a *true surplus*. The land produces more, an absolute increase, a bounty. This early school of economic thought thereby starkly identifies the concept of *surplus*, even if many of the assumptions on which their system was based prove incorrect.

2. Thomas Piketty and his colleagues have attempted to gather data on global economic growth rates going back to antiquity. While our approach here

would strictly question whether it is even possible to compare pre-capitalist and capitalist social orders in this way, this particular data set proves illuminating. According to Piketty's data, from the year 0000 to the year 1500 "growth" is effectively zero. Only, that is, after the first emergence of capitalist social orders does economic growth, economic surplus, become possible.

3. This, after all, is what excess revenue looks like: spreadsheet profit results can only occur if all costs spent on C (in various forms) add up to less than the total sales of C'.

4. Historically, of course, human beings have been bought and sold, have been *treated as* ownable and exchangeable commodities. As W. E. B. Du Bois powerfully shows, under certain modern forms of slavery, human beings have even been "produced" in order to be sold—as was the case in certain slave-breeding plantations in states like Virginia during the final decades of US legal slavery. "Chattel slavery" is the name given to a legal system that precisely defines (some) human beings as property and protects the rights of "property owners." To be clear, under such a legal system it is not *labor* that is treated as a commodity, but *human beings as such.* Chattel slavery is illegal everywhere in the world today. This legal status does not prevent other practices of forced servitude and domination to persist (general forms of "enslavement"), but it does render impossible the formal legal commodification of human beings.

5. It might be tempting to think of labor as general service commodity, but the labor contract is both like and unlike a service contract. When I buy an Uber ride, I pay for a specific service (and therefore a particular commodity)—for example, "take me from my home to the movie theater." When I hire a worker and pay them at an hourly rate, the worker is not selling a specific service; they are selling their labor-power. There is no concrete commodity being exchanged; rather, the wage contract treats labor itself like a purchasable commodity. This difference is subtle and can be blurred in practice: if I contract with a house painter to paint the exterior of my house for $2,000, then I'm buying a service commodity (the painting of my house); if I contract with a house painter to paint the exterior of my house by working at a rate of $20/hour, then I'm buying the painter's labor-power. Notice that the difference can be found in the contract itself: in the first case I am buying the painting of my house (the service); in the second I am hiring the work that will be used to paint my house (the labor-power).

6. As we emphasize here, labor-power is a peculiar and unique commodity. We must therefore take every care to be clear and precise about the meaning and use of this term. In everyday language we might use the phrase "labor

power" to refer to the generic capacity of someone to labor, their "power" to work. "Labor-power" names something entirely different; it names the *specific commodity exchanged in the wage contract* and used by the capitalist in production. Whenever we refer to this commodity we will always use the term "labor-power," and we will distinguish it from actual labor, on the one hand, and from the broad capacity to labor, on the other.

7. As we will explain in greater detail in Part III, *surplus value* (*SV*) is the *source* of capitalist profit (of net revenue), but it is not profit itself. Any concrete accounting profit is always a *cut* from the overall surplus value.

8. There is an important analogy between the market for labor-power (the wage relation) and the market for money (loans). In both cases the fundamental relation is a power relation that mirrors the social relations of money: the person with first-class credits also has power, and they can leverage that power to make more money. The banker does it by making loans and requiring the borrower to pay back more money. The enterprise owner does it by paying wages and paying the worker less than the value of his output. (With the wage relation, the worker gets paid *after* the work is done—unlike the borrower, who gets the money up front.)

PART III

CAPITALIST ECONOMIC FORCES

Part II zoomed in to provide fine-grained analysis of some of the central elements that make up a capitalist social order. By developing our conceptual understanding of money, commodities, and profit, we sharpened our overall view of capitalist economic relations. This focused theoretical work thus provides us with the apparatus required to take a wider view of contemporary, concrete capitalist social orders, and to understand the interconnections between economic forces and political, social, and cultural forces. Put much more bluntly: we are now prepared to explain what actually goes on in a capitalist system today.

What do capitalists actually *do*, and *why* and *how* do they do it? How do their actions relate to and impinge on the actions of workers, of citizens writ large, and of political actors? Now that we understand what money is, and now that we have grasped its centrality to a capitalist mode of production, how do we explain the role of money in contemporary society today? What does it mean to call the US dollar the "world reserve currency," and what are the implications of this fact? Now that we understand the strange metaphysical nature of the commodity, how do we make sense of the fact that the United States and Europe manufacture fewer commodities today than they did in the past, while China makes a growing proportion of the commodities sold throughout the world? If Google, Apple, and Facebook are all Silicon Valley "tech companies," what does it mean that Apple sells millions and millions of commodities, yet Google and Facebook do not? Now that we understand profit, how do we analyze the source of profits (and the different sizes of profits) for Google, Apple, and Facebook? How do we make sense of the fact that a sizable and growing chunk of profits in the American economy all go to financial firms? Why are all the best and brightest college graduates going to work on Wall Street or in Silicon Valley, and does it matter?

We will not address all of these questions directly in this part of the book, but we develop our framework for analysis of capitalist economics so that readers themselves have the conceptual toolkit needed to answer them—and we will explore a few of these examples as direct case studies. Along the way we will return to a point underscored in Part I but largely left in the background of Part II: economic forces and relations *never* operate in isolation or in a vacuum but rather always interact with, work against and alongside, sociopolitical forces and relations. This means that the specific answers to concrete "economic" questions will never be strictly economic; they will always prove to be "socioeconomic," "econopolitical," and so on.

It also means that the questions we take up in Part III will always be simultaneously both economic questions and questions of power relations (political questions). We will discover that there are certain fundamental problems in the history of economic thought that simply cannot be answered on restrictively economic grounds. If we want to understand the choices and actions of entrepreneurs, we can only do so within the context of a political and regulatory environment. If we want to understand the market for stocks, bonds, and derivatives, we have to take account of tax structures and broader political environments. Most pointedly, if we want to make sense of interest rates, we cannot ignore the fundamental fact that they always involve direct power relations. One way to express this broad point, which will be brought home again and again in this final part of the book, is to say that the concrete study of economics is always the study of *political economy*.

In the following three chapters we bring our introduction of *capitalist economics* to a close by taking a wider-angle view, while still retaining a focus on specific foregrounded elements. Chapter 7 considers one of the most-celebrated aspects of capitalism: entrepreneurship and the entrepreneur. We *situate* the entrepreneur within the context of a capitalist mode of production, making it possible for us to pose probing questions about the agency, role, and impact of entrepreneurs on the entire capitalist social order. Just as significantly, by broaching the issue of entrepreneurship, we concomitantly bring up the crucial questions of *capital* and *investment*. If the system is called "capitalism," then shouldn't we have a clarifying and concise definition of "capital"? To produce this definition requires understanding entrepreneurial agency, on the one hand, and distinguishing capital investment from money savings, on the other.

These analytic clarifications lead directly into Chapter 8, where we build on the discussion of money in Chapter 4 in order to make sense of contemporary banking and finance. The banker and the entrepreneur exist in a symbiotic but occasionally antagonistic relationship. It is impossible to understand one without the other, which means that each element in this pair presupposes and depends on the other. Here we reveal what banking practices actually look like; doing so utterly debunks orthodox economic theories of money. It also raises perhaps the hardest question in the history of economic thought: What is "the interest rate"?

Having tackled that question, and linked it to politics, we conclude the book in Chapter 9 with a survey of "the rules of capitalism." These are the primary economic forces in a capitalist social order. In the process of enumerating them we again clarify the central point of the book. These are *powerful* forces that exert massive shaping, structuring, and constraining effects on the entire society. It is therefore essential to see these forces as *economic forces*; they cannot be reduced to politics (or to social or cultural convention), and we ignore them at our peril. Nonetheless, they operate within and across a social order marked by distinct power relations, so the task of grasping capitalist economics requires attention to the interplay between and among all these forces.

7

Entrepreneurs and Investment

Sustaining Capitalism

We have now developed a detailed definition and analysis of the capitalist mode of production as the central element in "capitalism" as an overall social order. Nevertheless, our focused exploration of the capitalist circulatory system—the circulation of money and commodities for the goal of realizing a surplus (profit)—still leaves a number of crucial areas unexplored and unexplained. While we have a sense of how a capitalist social order comes about in terms of long historical development, and while we have a more incisive grasp of the fundamental capitalist economic relations, we still have not investigated the crucial question of *what causes the system to run*. That is, if we refer back to our code for capitalist production, we can clearly see that it begs an absolutely essential series of questions:

$$M \rightarrow C...P...C' \rightarrow M'$$

What starts the process? Where does the initial M come from in the first place? We have insisted throughout this book that there is nothing natural or inevitable about capitalist economics; a capitalist social order only first emerged in history because of changes in social, legal, and property relations that then, in turn, led both to the extended use of markets for capitalist purposes, and ultimately to the reorganization of production oriented toward the goal of market exchange for profit. Furthermore, we can now assert what should be obvious but is not often stated: capitalism is not a perpetual motion machine; once it has come into being, nothing guarantees that it will continue to run. So what makes capitalism go?

Capitalist Economics. Samuel A. Chambers, Oxford University Press. © Oxford University Press 2022.
DOI: 10.1093/oso/9780197556887.003.0008

Entrepreneurs: The Source of M

The answer can be found in the name itself: capitalism as an economic system hinges on the specific actions and the fundamental agency of *capitalists*. Up to this point in the book, in naming these central actors we have freely alternated between "enterprise owners" and "capitalists." The former emphasizes the practical work process: the organization and planning aspects, the idea of running a capitalist firm, arranging production, and projecting sales. The latter stresses the fundamental monetary basis: to be a capitalist it is necessary (but not sufficient) to have money that you are free to use in the pursuit of more money. Even in a capitalist social order, the vast majority of people are not and cannot be capitalists, either because they have no money or because the only money they have must be spent on basic life necessities (food, clothing, shelter).[1] When it comes to the crux of the matter that we are addressing here—the issue of *initiating* the circulatory process that is the capitalist mode of production—perhaps the best term is the French-borrowing "entrepreneur." The *Oxford English Dictionary*'s definition of entrepreneur nicely synthesizes our two previous terms: "A person who owns and manages a business, bearing the financial risks of the enterprise." An entrepreneur is a capitalist enterprise owner.

The continued existence of capitalism always depends, elementally and inherently, on the actions of entrepreneurs. If money is not "advanced" to begin with, then capitalist production does not occur. To expand on this idea, it can help to reiterate what occurs in this process. It actually starts in exchange: the entrepreneur begins the process by throwing money into circulation, by purchasing commodities (means of production and labor-power) on the market. These initial purchases then allow the entrepreneur to begin the concrete process of production, the process by which the initial C (raw materials) gets transformed into C' (finished goods). At this juncture we should stress a point that we mostly skipped over in the previous chapter: in order for the capitalist system to continue running smoothly, in order for the process to continue, the value of C' (which includes surplus value within it) must be *realized on the market*. Under capitalism, value is only realized, only concretely manifested, when it takes the form of money. We call someone rich because of the totals in their bank accounts, not because they own factories that have filled warehouses with unsold products. The finished goods must find willing buyers in possession of money. If they do not—if value is not realized by commodities being sold—then the entire process was for naught since the entrepreneur will find herself not with the intended goal, more money, but instead with less money and with a bunch of unsellable commodities (with effectively no exchange-value).

We can reformulate this point as follows: the continued running of the capitalist system depends not only on the actions and choices of entrepreneurs (to use their money to initiate production) but also on **the expectations entrepreneurs have about the possible realization of value** (sales of commodities) at the end of the process. We previously underscored the fact that unlike exchange (which happens roughly instantaneously), production is a temporal process that happens over a fixed and often lengthy period. Now we can complicate that argument by seeing that capitalist production is also *futural*, meaning that it depends on projections and expectations about the future. The **generation of surplus value occurs in production, but the realization of surplus value always depends on exchange**—it is always sustained by market demand. So much so that the initial M (and thus the initial C) are both themselves determined by the expectation (on the part of the entrepreneur) of how much C' can be realized in exchange.

At the beginning of each potential production process, the entrepreneur must decide whether to advance the initial M. This decision is the spark for the entire capitalist engine; or, to continue our previous vascular system metaphor, we can say that entrepreneurs are the pacemakers for capitalism because their choices determine whether the heart (capitalist production) beats and the blood (money and commodities) flows.[2] A deeper understanding of capitalism requires us to explore further the many elements in, and implications of, this decision.

Capital Investment

In everyday discourse we hear the word "investment" used interchangeably to describe both the entrepreneurial choice to advance money for capitalist production and the decision to place excess cash in various financial securities with the expectation that they will increase in value. A "security" is usually defined as a "financial instrument"—that is, a form of money-credit—that can be divided neatly into three categories of "equities" (i.e., stocks), "debts" (e.g., certificates of deposit, bonds), and derivatives (contracts with money value that are traded). This means that everyone from wealth managers to financial planners to the business press will use the word "investment" to mean *buying securities* (putting money into a different form of money), while that same business press and others will also use the word "investment" to mean *expanding production*.

The everyday discourse proves problematic, then, because we want to draw as stark a distinction as possible between these two broad categories of "investment." Indeed, when it comes to understanding the key action of entrepreneurs as the pacemakers of capitalism, **buying raw materials and buying a bond prove to be totally opposite actions**. We will deal with financial securities in greater detail in the next chapter, but for now we can focus on a more direct point: if an entrepreneur takes their extra money and uses it to buy a stock, then they are actively *not* choosing to use that money to initiate *their own* capitalist production process.

We can extend this example in a way that helps clear up a related confusion over the term "investment." If I have $1 million and use it to buy computer components (MP) and to hire laborers (LP) to assemble those components into smartphones, then I have clearly advanced M ($1 million worth). After assembly I will wind up with C' in the form of a whole bunch of smartphones, and I will market them for sale at a total market price of $1.2 million. If they all sell at the market price, I will realize $200,000 in profit (derived from the surplus value created in production).

But what if I take the initial $1 million and buy Apple stock? Many commentators on capitalism frequently suggest that this act is also capital investment. Indeed, people who trade on the stock market are commonly referred to as *investors*. This is not for nothing; the idea here is that in buying Apple stock, I have made $1 million available for Tim Cook to initiate the production of more iPhones. Nevertheless, this logic will not hold because my purchase of stock does not directly begin the process of producing iPhones. Yes, it is a theoretical

possibility that Tim Cook *could* use my money to add to iPhone production, but he could also just add it to Apple's $200 billion stockpile
of cash on hand (as of late 2019). He could use it to fund a dividend
paid out to shareholders. He could give bonuses to his VPs. He could
do whatever he wants with my money, but ultimately the decision has
now been passed off from me to Tim Cook (and as the numbers here
indicate, Tim Cook hardly needs my $1 million). Perhaps Apple will
eventually increase capital investment, but that is a separate question, a
separate temporal decision to advance M or not. Regardless, *I have not
advanced M when I buy Apple stock.*

In general, **money spent on a security is not** M (the first term in
our code for capitalist production). We will therefore distinguish rigorously from here on out between the use of money to purchase financial securities (in any form) and the direct use of money to purchase
production commodities (MP and LP) as the initiation of a production
process. Only the latter should be considered *capital investment.* To
be clear, in this book we will typically refer to it using our own termi-
nology, as the advancement of M. In the next chapter we will explore
in more detail a crucial point raised here: the initiation of production
processes hinges on whether entrepreneurs expect a greater return
from production or from the appreciation of securities. Put simply, if
expected return on capital investment is lower than the guaranteed return on government bonds, the capitalist economy is in big trouble.
Hence Chapter 8 will return to the central agent of capitalist production, the entrepreneur. But now we want to take a different turn, to
show that though the capitalist lives and acts at the very nucleus of capitalism, the system cannot run on capitalists alone.

Workers: The Source of LP

We have now underlined a point often made in everyday discussions
about politics and economics: capitalism depends on the actions
and choices of entrepreneurs, particularly their willingness to advance money (M) to initiate the production process. But as we have
shown repeatedly in this book, the capitalist mode of production

proves complex and dynamic, made possible by multiple interrelated elements. For example, in this chapter we have begun with the entrepreneur's advancement of a sum of money (M), but we should not forget that such an action requires and presupposes the existence of a viable monetary system. There is no entrepreneur without a system of money: a social system of reliable credit and debt that makes it possible for the entrepreneur to purchase raw materials and labor-power. This point can be driven home with more force when we consider that today almost all new workers are hired, contracted for wage labor, and put to work, all based on nothing more than a *promise to pay* from the employer.[3] A stable monetary system and a reliable payments and processing system prove essential to contemporary capitalist production.

Turning again to the entrepreneur, we see that he will need more than money. The entrepreneur must find the elements needed to carry out production available for sale on the market. As we have noted, these are the overall commodities (C) that are used in production, and they can be broken down into the constituent elements—means of production (MP) and labor-power (LP). We can therefore create a long list of ways that the capitalist engine might grind to a halt: a shortage in the means of production, whether it be machines or raw materials, will at best lead to a slowdown in production, and at worst to a stoppage. Formulated in more general terms, we see that **the production of all commodities depends on the production of all other commodities**; as a system of circulation of money and commodities, all parts of the capitalist social order are connected (directly or indirectly).

But as we have shown in detail in Chapter 6, labor-power is a special commodity, a unique commodity, and it plays a fundamental role in capitalism. All capitalist production relies on the existence and availability of labor-power. Imagine an entrepreneur who goes into business manufacturing special-use lithium-ion batteries. After a brief period of success, she runs into a supply problem: due to global shortages, to environmental regulations, or to tariff wars, she can no longer access the market for a key chemical component in battery production. This forces a change in our entrepreneur's practices: she might rework the chemical makeup of her batteries, she might alter her production process to source premade batteries that she then modifies, or, faced with no other viable options, she might cease battery production entirely.

But even in this worst-case scenario, our entrepreneur does not have to stop being an entrepreneur: she could switch to another business entirely. After all, the overall production process does not depend on any *particular* process for the production of commodities, only on money. And assuming she has not gone bankrupt, our entrepreneur can go into a different line of business.

However, this optimistic scenario will not hold if labor-power is unavailable on the market. **Without labor-power, no production processes can be undertaken.** We must remind ourselves exactly what this means, so that we can grasp the reality of this potential problem. If we make the mistake of confusing labor-power with "labor" or the *capacity* to labor, then we would obviously conclude that we can never run out of it (as long as there are human beings, there is the capacity to labor). Yet labor-power, as we showed in detail in Chapter 6, must not be conflated with the general human ability to work; labor-power is the unique capitalist commodity, and it only appears as a commodity when workers agree to wage contracts—agree to "sell their labor-power." In the world we live in today, this fact, the fact of ubiquitous wage labor, seems like a given, a natural condition of the world. But we know from a brief glance at history that it's nothing of the sort: prior to the rise of capitalism, wage labor did indeed exist, but it was sporadic and limited; it was not at all the dominant form of work. Beyond history, we can also see in conceptual terms why the availability of labor-power cannot be guaranteed.

To do so, let's take the example that often appears in political, economic, and cultural discourse today as the capitalist dream: the ideal society in which everyone is an entrepreneur. Imagine that everyone is a Silicon Valley startup founder. This example is surely a fantasy because it requires us to describe a world in which all human beings are rich enough that they do not immediately have to work for a wage in order to survive. Everyone has enough extra money available that they can feed, clothe, and shelter themselves, and they have access to enough money besides that they can choose to invest in capitalist production. But as far-fetched as that assumption might be (the assumption of global wealth for everyone), that is not even the biggest problem with this case. The problem runs deeper: **if literally everyone in the world decides to make money by being a capitalist,** then capitalism ceases to exist. Why? Because in such a scene labor-power disappears as an available capitalist commodity. None of our entrepreneurs can purchase labor-power, so none can initiate a production process—hence none can make money. If total capitalism means everyone is a capitalist, then **total capitalism means the end of capitalism**.

The capitalist mode of production can only be sustained if a huge percentage of individuals *lack* the ability to purchase means of production and therefore *need to work for a wage in order to live*. Here we see with clarity the often confused idea of "class." Regardless of whether entrepreneurs seem relatively "poor" and workers seem relatively "rich," we can always distinguish, in capitalism, between entrepreneurs (who can choose to initiate production processes, or choose *not* to initiate such processes) and workers (who may or may not be able to choose *where* they work, but definitely cannot choose *not* to work).

This means, perhaps counterintuitively, that the entrepreneur's existence and success depend upon the existence of the worker. **If there are no workers there can be no entrepreneurs, and in turn, there can be no capitalism.** Throughout history this basic fact of capitalism has often manifested in significant "extra-economic" (that is, political and cultural) efforts by the entrepreneurial strata of society to create conditions in which labor-power was consistently available as a commodity. It also explains why the primary *political* power wielded by workers as a class manifests in their capacity (or lack thereof) to withhold labor-power from the market (particularly through strikes, but also in the form of working-day limitations, worker-safety regulations, paid time off, etc.).[4] But finally, this analysis also gives us a clear sense of why any power struggle between workers and capitalists will never be carried out on a level playing field. In order to truly remove labor-power from the market (the one real blow workers can lodge against capitalists) workers must refuse to work and thereby give up their wages. Yet the basic condition of being a worker in the first place is to need a wage in order to survive, so workers could ultimately destroy capitalists (and capitalism) only at the risk of first destroying themselves.

Capitalism and Inequality

This analysis raises much bigger and conceptually complex questions about the very nature of capitalism and its past and future historical trajectories. We know from a study of history what it means for one dominant mode of production to replace another. Feudalism was a long-developed mode of production when capitalism (that is, first the increasing capitalist use of markets and then the unique reorganization of production according to capitalist principles) began to erode its foundations. But we really do not have any historical examples of an advanced capitalist mode of production being replaced. Typically cited cases of modern "noncapitalist" countries—the Soviet Union, China under Mao Zedong, Cuba—are all instances of a noncapitalist social order developing out of a precapitalist system, and doing so within a context of global capital. We do not really know what a full transition *out of capitalism* might look like. Perhaps this is why some commentators who are most staunchly devoted to capitalism see it as the "final" historical form of a social order; they believe that historical development inevitably leads all societies to become capitalist social orders—that there are no alternatives.

However, our example above, where everyone in the world is an entrepreneur, already proves that capitalist progress cannot be unlimited in the sense that these commentators have suggested. Capitalism cannot make everyone rich, because the capitalist mode of production depends fundamentally on the existence of a majority class of people who sell their labor-power as a commodity on the exchange market (and rich people need not work for a wage in order to survive).

Today we hear many arguments about the ways in which capitalism contributes to socioeconomic inequality in terms of concrete practical results—for example, because CEO pay, financial gains on securities, and other elements of what Thomas Piketty captures in his "rate of return" variable, are increasing faster than measures of overall economic growth. And this means that the accumulation of wealth (in the form of money, of course) quickly outstrips any possible increases to wage income. Piketty expresses this conundrum through the literary motif wherein a person not born into wealth has only one real option to become wealthy: marrying into it. Our own, deeper structural analysis of how a capitalist mode of production functions allows us to make a different point than the one Piketty draws from empirical observation. Regardless of the outcomes of the running of the capitalist system (this is what Piketty's data *measures*), we can already see that as an overall system of production, distribution, and exchange, as a structuring principle for an entire social order, **capitalism depends on, for its very conditions of existence, a fundamental inequality.**[5] Not everyone can be a capitalist, and capitalists can never be economically equal to workers, since the basic difference between them is that one has access to an M they can advance (money) and the other does not.

What Is Capital?

With our central finding that not everyone can be a capitalist, we have reached a significant conclusion with manifold implications. The capitalist mode of production can only come into being and can only continue to exist if some people have access to an M they can advance, while some other people *lack that very same access* and therefore have no choice but to enter into wage contracts (the legal structure that gives rise to labor-power as a commodity). A concise way of stating this point, in a language we could have used from the start of this chapter, is to say that capitalists have access to *capital* and workers do not. But what is capital?

It might seem surprising that we have waited until the end of Chapter 7 to consider the definition of capital since it must be *a*, if not *the*, central term in this book. But this is not by chance. We have waited for a reason: while *capital* does prove to be an absolutely essential term, it cannot be defined in advance of our broad and rigorous analysis of a capitalist mode of production and its fundamental elements and concepts. Most importantly, capital is not an empirical object. **We cannot define capital *ostensively***—that is, by pointing to its occurrence or appearance in the world (or in history). Capital is not an empirical thing. We cannot understand it by trying to count it. Indeed, although attempts to *measure* capital can prove very important for our understanding of a capitalist social order, those very attempts are never simple or straightforward, but always fraught (always complicated and subject to skeptical questioning).

Of course, most standard accounts of capital do define it empirically, as a "factor of production," a produced item such as tools, equipment, or machinery. Often such accounts use the phrase capital *stock* to indicate precisely the idea that capital names physical items in the world. This notion is sometimes contrasted with "flows" that indicate *changes* in quantities or refer to monetary measures. In general these definitions of capital as capital goods call to mind factories and warehouses filled with tools, production implements, and other material items.

Such definitions are not wrong per se. Indeed, these textbook accounts often provide concrete *examples* of capital; nonetheless, they fail to *define* capital, and they come up profoundly short in providing any conceptual understanding of capital. The problem can be stated as follows: the examples given (as definitions) *might be* examples of capital, but they also *might not be*. By defining capital empirically, standard accounts *assume* that we will identify capital in and of itself, as an object we observe in the world. The problem here is that sometimes a thing is capital, and sometimes it is not. **Capital is not a thing, but a thing can be capital.** (This is why the texts offer only examples and not rigorous definitions.) The key question then becomes: *When is a thing capital and when is it not?*

To answer, let's start by pointing out something you may have already observed: the standard ostensive definitions of capital all seem to be pointing to the first *C* in our code for the capitalist mode of production. Assume as our example a Tesla car factory: standard accounts would identify a robot that installs a door onto the frame of a car as the "capital." Is the robot capital? Our initial answer: *probably*.

However, in order to know for sure, we have to look harder—we have to widen our view beyond a frozen single image of the robot itself. We therefore start with the overall code:

$$M \to C...P...C' \to M'$$

We can then quickly work our way through a basic checklist:

- Elon Musk is the entrepreneur who advanced the initial M.
- The door-installing robot is a part of the C purchased with that M.
- The robot installs 47 doors per day in an online (currently operating) factory in California that produces 300 Model 3 cars per day.
- Tesla is currently turning over (selling) all of their inventory.
- Last quarter Tesla made a small profit (net revenue).

Having gone through our list—that is, having placed the robot into the context of a capitalist process of production—we can reach a final answer: yes, the door-installing robot is capital.

But our answer proves far more subtle and complex since there are many other dimensions of it. To start with, the initial sum of money that Musk advanced is also capital. What about the finished Model 3 cars available for sale? Yes, they are capital too. And the revenue generated by the sales of those cars? Yep, also capital. However, the Model 3 that has been delivered to the Silicon Valley software developer, which he drives to work to show off to his friends: that commodity has already been purchased (its value realized) and it now becomes a consumption good (used not in production but for practical enjoyment by the software developer). Once the car is purchased, it is no longer capital. And if Elon Musk decides to remove the door-installing robot from the factory floor and take it home to work on a hobby for his own personal amusement, the minute the robot leaves the factory floor, it ceases to be capital.

Capital is not a single thing or set of things. **Capital is a relation.** That is, capital is any *element*—money or commodities—*within an active capitalist process of production.* Any entity (commodity or money) actively taking on the role of M, C, C', or M' is capital.[6] Yet when the same entity exits the system (and moves outside of that production process), it ceases to be capital. Importantly, this means that the end of each production process, the moment at which value is realized as M', proves critical. If that sum of money is thrown back into circulation (to buy production commodities) then it starts another production process and continues to circulate as capital, but if it is withdrawn from circulation (used to buy a vacation for the entrepreneur) then it no longer functions as capital. To borrow David Harvey's phrase, capital is "value in motion." **Capital is money and/or commodities as they circulate in a capitalist process of production.** This means that not all money and commodities are capital, and some money/commodities that are capital at one time will cease to be capital at a future time. Money and commodities are capital if and only if they are part of the process of capitalist production.

Money Capital

We close this chapter by observing the tight connection between our definition of capital as an element in the process of value production and realization, on the one hand, and our sharp distinction between the purchase of securities and the advancement of M, on the other. The rich conceptual language that we have now developed allows us to say succinctly: buying bonds and stocks might be a form of "investment" in the sense of savings, but it is decidedly not *capital investment*. We now have a framework to indicate that money is sometimes capital and sometimes not: when money is moved from a bank account to a certificate of deposit, or used to purchase a bond, that money does not change form—it remains a financial asset. In contrast, when money is advanced for capitalist production, that money is/becomes capital, and can therefore be fairly categorized as a form of investment (*capital* investment). This account brings us to the crux of the matter in that this radical difference (between investing and not investing) comes down to a basic question: What does the entrepreneur choose to do with her money? And we cannot even begin to answer that question before exploring *the business of money* in more detail.

Notes

1. The idea of "human capital" suggests that spending money on yourself, especially for things like education or technical training, can be understood as a form of investment, an "investment in yourself." Our analysis will define investment much more rigorously. Understood from the perspective of

capitalist production, a student who goes into debt to earn a degree needed for being hired as a worker is not "investing" but rather subsidizing the costs of the capitalist who employs him.

2. Technically, because they can both start and stop the process, entrepreneurs are ICDs: implantable cardioverter defibrillators, fancier versions of the old-tech pacemaker.

3. In this context we should also clarify that while the standard phrase is that money is "advanced" by the entrepreneur, we know from real-world practices that the term is deceptive. The capitalist does typically advance money to purchase means of production (production commodities available for sale on the exchange market), but when it comes to labor-power, the worker in fact "advances" her labor-power to the capitalist. Actual wages are only paid afterwards. One simple but insightful way to track the power relations between economic actors in a capitalist social order is by checking the temporal lag and directionality of payment. For example, renters pay monthly rent in advance; homeowners pay their mortgage at the end of the month. Some workers are paid at the end of each week, while some are not paid until the end of the month. If you do the interest-rate math, you can see that for a large corporation the difference between weekly and monthly payment of wages can total in the tens or hundreds of thousands of dollars.

4. Workers also negotiate for better economic conditions in the form of higher wages and benefits, though these bargains actually help to preserve the general availability of labor-power on the market.

5. This is certainly an "economic" inequality since it manifests most directly in money terms, but throughout history it has also been expressed in, and been maintained by, a panoply of social, cultural, and political inequalities (e.g., property or capital requirements for voting). Put simply, one way for a social order to ensure the availability of labor-power is to create laws and norms that, in various ways, require it.

6. Production, ...P... , is not capital since it is not a "thing" at all, but rather a complex and dynamic process.

8

Bankers and Interest

Making Money

To understand the role of bankers, stock brokers, and a whole panoply of other agents involved in the financial industry, we first need to
take a step back and reconsider the central question of surplus value
and profit that we analyzed in Chapter 6. We must foreground a crucial point that was implicitly assumed in that chapter. We showed how
surplus value is generated by a capitalist production process, but this
process is not confined to a single firm or even a single nation: the capitalist mode of production's generation of surplus value occurs on a
global scale. The Apple iPhone may well be "designed in California,"
but the supply chains (means of production) and workforce (labor-
power) involved in its manufacture include a dozen or more countries
stretching across the globe.

Apple's net revenue (accounting profit) is not directly equivalent or
even proportional to its generation of surplus value. Entrepreneurs organize, plan, initiate, and carry out capitalist production in order to
realize profit. But individual entrepreneurs do not receive the specific
amount of surplus value generated in their industry any more than
the poker players in our imaginary surplus-value poker game would
each receive "their share" of surplus value. Recall that in our example
most poker players were still net losers, but because of surplus value,
the winners won larger sums such that the total cashed out was higher
than the original buy-in. Any individual firm's net revenue profits are
always a distribution (a *cut*) from the overall sum of surplus value generated globally by the capitalist mode of production (see Figure 1).[1]

This leads us to a key deduction: the fact that surplus value is
redistributed (across firms, across nation-states) means that **a capitalist social order presents many opportunities to *make profits* (in
the sense of net revenue) *without actually generating any surplus***

Capitalist Economics. Samuel A. Chambers, Oxford University Press. © Oxford University Press 2022.
DOI: 10.1093/oso/9780197556887.003.0009

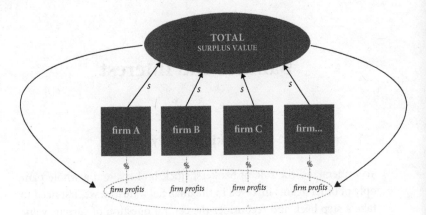

Figure 1 The global production and distribution of surplus value.

value. In other words, our analysis in Chapter 6 explained how surplus value arises within a global capitalist system of production, and therefore described surplus value as the *source* of profit for any particular industry or enterprise. But that analysis did not touch a broader clutch of questions about the distribution of surplus value. One way to make money in capitalism is to be an entrepreneur—and without entrepreneurs and workers, capitalism cannot be sustained—but it is not the only way, and arguably it isn't even the "best" (i.e., easiest) way. To get a wider sense of the overall capitalist social order, we have to expand our analysis to include agents (and related sectors) of the social order who are, strictly speaking, neither workers nor capitalists.

Rent

Landlords and rent provide the oldest example. Most entrepreneurs require a location—a space, *land* of some sort—on which to conduct the business of their enterprise. They could, of course, buy the land outright, but any *M* sunk into land purchase is *M* unavailable for advancement as capitalist investment.[2] Therefore most entrepreneurs rent their land (lease their space). What, then, is rent, and how do landlords and rent payments fit into the capitalist code? The most

Profit and Surplus Value: The Case of Advertising

As we showed in detail in Chapter 6, surplus value does not show up on any accounting spreadsheets (because ΔM is not directly measurable), nor does it appear in corporations' filings with the US Securities and Exchange Commission. All we can find in those documents is an entry for "net income" (another term for net revenue). In other words, we only ever observe *profit* directly, not surplus value, which we understand is the very source of profit.

Because profit is all we see, we tend to relate capitalist firms to one another solely on this metric, and we usually completely fail to see that one firm's profit (net revenue) may only be possible on the basis of other firms' generation of surplus value. For example, today's most famous American corporations seem very similar because they all post massive revenues and they are all technology companies. Ranked by profit over the past four quarters, Apple ($57B), Google/Alphabet ($37B), Facebook ($22B), and Amazon ($17B) look very much alike. But these numbers do not answer—in fact, they may mask—more important questions about how much overall economic activity these firms generate and, most importantly, *where their profits come from.*

Amazon, for example, is last on the list when ranked by profit, but when ranked by overall revenue generated they come first, with $280B compared to Facebook's $80B. An even more striking contrast is revealed when we see that Apple's number one revenue source is the iPhone, accounting for 50 percent of their total revenue of $260B, while Facebook's primary source of revenue is advertising, which accounts for an amazing 98 percent of their total. Facebook and Apple may both be "tech companies," but Facebook doesn't make money from producing technological goods or services. In terms of sources of revenue and profit, Facebook is not a tech company; they are an advertising company.

Moreover, the "sale" of advertising (in contrast with the work done by ad agencies to create ads) is much more like the rental of land than it is the production of commodities. To make iPhones, Apple engages in capitalist production (paying for *MP* and *LP* to produce and sell a commodity) that generates surplus value. In selling advertising, Facebook generates almost no surplus value at all.

important answers we can give are the following negatives: **rent is not capital, and rent is not surplus value.** Rent is a cost that precedes our initial C, and it can therefore only be paid as a cut out of our final M'. The landowner, the person to whom the entrepreneur pays rent, is therefore not an entrepreneur himself; he simply leverages his property rights in order to extract a portion of the entrepreneur's net revenue, which itself comes out of the larger fund of surplus value produced by the capitalist mode of production globally. Notice that land does not "generate" an income (rent) naturally or inherently (the vast majority of the globe is unused for any productive purposes[3]); rather, only under specific circumstances within capitalism does the title to land give the landlord the opportunity to receive a cut of the surplus generated by the capitalist mode of production. For the landowner, the entrepreneur's need for space is a stroke of great luck; for the entrepreneur, rent is the price of doing business.

$M \rightarrow M'$ (Again)

Previous chapters have made plain that land is not the element the entrepreneur most depends on. By definition **the capitalist must have money**—the initial M that begins the production process. This fact creates one of the biggest opportunities for money-making in a capitalist social order. We started our historical analysis of capitalism with a discussion of the capitalist use of markets, where one starts with money in an effort to obtain more money, $M \rightarrow M'$. We can now return to that formula to see that under capitalism, money can be used almost directly to make more money when it takes the form of interest-bearing capital—that is, when a banker lends money to an entrepreneur. The entrepreneur then throws the lent sum into capitalist production, where (she hopes) it will produce a surplus, out of which she will pay the banker back the interest owed. For the entrepreneur, interest paid to the banker looks just like rent paid to the landlord, and as we will see, interest is best understood as a form of rent (rent on money). For the banker, who is not involved in and may not even see the capitalist production process, it would appear that money simply grows out of money. Banking revenue and financial profits are all like rent: they are a cut taken out of the overall surplus value generated elsewhere. Moreover, today these "industries" play a large role in the overall capitalist system; their actions have massive consequences for capitalist social orders as a whole. No understanding of capitalist economics would be complete without at least a broader overview of their role, function, and structure.

Banks and Bankers

"Banker" is the broad name for the agent in capitalism who takes on, as a vocation, the practice of using money to make more money. We can start with the purest form of "banking," where this means lending money at interest in order to directly generate more money. Unlike earlier (precapitalist) "merchant capitalists," who used arbitrage opportunities or trade routes to earn "profits" in a zero-sum game, the *capitalist banker* acts much more like the capitalist landlord. The banker uses his structural position within a capitalist social order in order to take a cut from the overall surplus value produced by the system. It should go without saying then that bankers are in the business of making money, but it is worth repeating the point since it helps to expose the fallacy we mentioned in Chapter 4—namely, the idea that banks are institutions designed to serve as "intermediaries" between borrowers and savers.

Banks are not public utilities; **banks are profit-maximizing firms within a capitalist social order.** How do banks make money? By making loans. Banks do not wait around for "savers" to "deposit money" that the banks can then "lend out." The process starts with bankers making loans as a basic form of business activity. Recall the crucial point from Chapter 4: loans are bank assets. My debt to the bank is the bank's credit against me. Moreover, money creation in a modern economy occurs precisely when banks make loans. Money creation is not external to the capitalist circulation of money and commodities. Money is not mined from the earth or "printed" by a central bank; money creation happens *endogenously* through economic action (entrepreneurs making commodities) and financial action (bankers making loans). The keystrokes that create the loan also generate new money in the economy, or as many commentators put it, "loans create deposits" in that when the bank gives me a loan or credit line, I immediately have credits in an account that I can spend (i.e., I have money).

At its core then, the reason for being and the primary function of a bank is to use money to make money, and since banks have the power to create money by initiating loans, they therefore also have enormous capacities for making money. But it proves crucial to underscore the point that this power of banks does not come out of thin air; it depends on the wider capitalist social order. All of the other work we have done in the book up to now helps us to see how this is possible in the first place: the nature of the capitalist production process (which generates surplus value) creates opportunities for other businesses to prosper on the basis of carving out a small portion of that value to be distributed to them. So we already know what bankers (and other financial-industry actors) do in the broadest sense: they make money off of money. But now we need to pose the harder question: *How do they do it?* What is the specific mechanism, and how does it function?

Interest Rates and Money

In one sense the answer seems simple: banks make money by charging a rate of interest on the money they loan out; other financial agents earn money by charging a fee that is itself a percentage of the interest earned on a portfolio of financial assets. But the easy answer only hides harder questions: What, exactly, is an interest rate, and what determines it? Traditionally interest rates have been defined (and thus explained away) quite simply as *the price of money*. On the model of banks as intermediaries there is *one* interest rate, and it is the rate that balances the supply of funds offered by savers with the demand for funds requested by borrowers. Banks just provide a location (perhaps virtual) where borrowers and savers can meet, and "the" interest is just like the price of a commodity—the equilibrium point where supply and demand intersect.

We have already undermined the idea of banks and bankers as neutral parties that help coordinate the actions of borrowers and savers; banks do not *first* attract deposits that they hold, only *then* to lend them out. Rather, they start their business by making loans. But that only barely begins the list of what's wrong with this model of interest rates as the price of money. Let us specify:

1. *Money is not a commodity.*
   Our analysis from Chapter 5 provides a rigorous account of the nature and structure of commodities. Commodities are two-fold entities; they are both use-values and exchange-values. But money does not meet these conditions. Unlike a hamburger or a hammer, money has no direct, intrinsic use-value. I can, of course, "use" money, but that involves a social system of coordination (of at least three parties) in which I transfer credits. Alone on a desert island (à la Robinson Crusoe) I can always eat my hamburger, but money is useless in isolation. While we might say that money has "exchange-value" in the sense that it can be swapped with commodities in particular ratios, there is no such thing as "the price" of money.

2. *Money has no value.*
   Money is *denomination*, the *measure* of exchange-value. **Commodities *have values* that are measured in money—but money *has no value*; money only measures the value of other things.** As a form of exchange-value that can circulate independently of use-value, money is the very embodiment of exchange-value, and thus price. But for that very reason, as the measure of value, money does not have value itself. As we showed in Chapter 4, money is credit/debt; money instruments (e.g., coins and notes) are tokens of debt that circulate. But those tokens have no value in themselves. Money measures value but does not have value, in the same way that meters, as the *measure* of length, do not have a length. This means that if we understand price as "measure of value," then strictly speaking money does not have a price. It therefore proves impossible for interest rates to be "the price of money."[4]

3. *There is no single interest rate.*
   The idea that there could be a single "interest rate" in the same way that markets for commodities are thought to have a "single price" proves seductive. It simplifies so much in other economic

analysis if we can always assume "the" interest rate.[5] No matter how enticing, the idea of a single interest rate never holds in practice. The evidence is overwhelming: credit card rates ranging from 12 to 30 percent; car loan rates ranging from 0 to 25 percent; savings rates from 0 to 1.9 percent. This list could go on forever. But it's important to be clear: rates vary, sometimes dramatically, even in those areas where interest rates are mostly highly regulated and measured in order to ensure supposed consistency.[6]

It is crucial to emphasize that in foreign exchange markets and other money markets (which are crucial features of contemporary capitalism), one currency can have an exchange rate with another. In this sense the "price" of 1 USD can be 0.737 GBP. But this ratio at which we swap one money-credit for another does not entail the same meaning of price that we would apply to the measure of a commodity's value. Interest rates simply are not the price of money in the standard sense in which we say $299 is the price of a Sony PlayStation. However, interest can still be rightly understood as a charge or a fee, since obviously a loan involves party A "charging interest" in the form of money to party B. That monetary charge is payment not for "buying" money (which makes no sense) but for *borrowing* it. This explanation brings into clear focus the key point: **interest is like rent**—it is the fee you pay for the use of something you do not own. Once we start to view interest rates as rental rates, we open the door to a wider understanding of interest rates and their role in a capitalist mode of production.

Interest Rates and Power

If we cannot develop or implement a model of "the" interest rate based on the economic modeling of commodity prices, then what can we say about interest rates? Interest rates are highly complicated, and we will not presume to unravel all their secrets here, but we can take a very important and positive first step by insisting on a point that has been foundational to everything we do in this book: interest rates are not strictly "economic." Interest rates reflect a set of power relations, and as power relations ebb and flow, so interest rates will increase and decrease. There's a kernel of truth in many bad banker jokes, and in broad strokes the answer to our primary question looks like a punchline. How much will a banker charge a customer who wants a loan? *As much as he can.*

Any banker will maximize revenue by maximizing interest charges, but this means that we can only compute the interest rate if we make not only economic (or budgetary) calculations but also legal, social, and political calculations. Undoubtedly, economic forces will limit rates, because for certain customers (on certain loans), one banker has to worry about another banker stealing their customer by offering better terms. But the final rate also depends on regulatory restrictions (throughout history certain interest rates—and in some instances all interest in general—have been designated illegal) and on the social status of the customer. Check-cashing institutions charge anywhere from 1 to 12 percent, just to give a person access to the funds they already earned. The average annual interest rate charged on payday loans in the United States is currently 391 percent. There is simply no amount of sophisticated economic analysis or mathematical modeling that can explain this rate or reconcile it with a theory of "one" interest rate.

We therefore gain a sharper view of the nature of banking, interest, and money in a capitalist social order if we view the financial industry through two lenses. First, we must always keep in mind that "financial services" never generate surplus. They only access a slice of a surplus produced elsewhere in the global economy. Second, we should consider the choices and actions of bankers and banks in terms of a broader structure of power relations in society. The capacity of bankers to make money off of money (and the amount they make) will always depend on their structural leverage. Fundamentally, a banker has money and offers it for a period of time to someone who needs it.

As an economic transaction, making and receiving a loan is nothing like purchasing a commodity. In a typical economic exchange of goods or services, the buyer (the person who pays) offers money in exchange for a commodity that they immediately receive. But with a loan, the person who is paying is the person who lacks money. Therefore loaning money must be understood as a special type of economic transaction in that the buyer is always at a disadvantage. That is, in normal economic exchange each party has something the other one wants: the seller has a commodity (i.e., a use-value) and the buyer has money (i.e., quality credits held on a third party). But in the loan transaction, the banker holds all the cards. We can therefore see that even from a narrowly "economic" viewpoint, the business of banking has distinct characteristics—power relations favor the seller (the banker).

Interest Rates and Entrepreneurs

Now that we have a clearer view of the function of bankers within a capitalist social order and of the nature of interest rates, we need to double back briefly and fold this analysis into our discussion of entrepreneurs and investment from the last chapter. Because the interest rate is not a natural market price but a social and political force, bankers and banking play an enormous role in capitalism. They do so by way of their massive impact on the decisions and choices of entrepreneurs. Indeed, we are now in a position to go beyond our analysis in Chapter 7, which showed us the structural role of entrepreneurs in a capitalist mode of production; we can now sketch out an explication of the decision-making of entrepreneurs.

At any given moment in time, each entrepreneur has to decide what to do with available money (M), and the basic choices reduce down to three:

1. Buy more commodities (C) for personal consumption (thereby destroying them).
2. Advance M to initiate the production process; that is, buy C in the form of MP and LP in order to produce C' that is then sold to realize M'.
3. Buy a financial asset in hopes the asset will appreciate.

We can safely ignore number 1 for three reasons: (a) in the social order as a whole, the amount of M spent on consumption goods proves minor compared to the scale of M committed to the other two categories; (b) the amount in this category gets expressed as basic consumer demand for market commodities elsewhere in our understanding of capitalist production and exchange, so it is already accounted for; and most importantly, (c) the entrepreneur, by definition, cannot spend all her money on consumption, since if she did she would no longer be an entrepreneur.

Hence the key decision is a binary one: does the entrepreneur *invest* (in the full sense of capitalist investment) or does she merely *save* (by purchasing financial assets)? In a sense the decision seems uncomplicated because both choices can be expressed in the same simple terms: $\Delta M / M$. What our entrepreneur wants and needs to know is the prospective rate of return on the M advanced, and this is what $\Delta M / M$ expresses. In the case of capitalist production, it is the ratio of net revenue to total costs, otherwise known as the profit rate. In the case of the financial asset, it is more directly the rate of return, or in the specific case of a bond, it is nothing other than the interest rate. Of course, these rates of return are always *probabilistic projections* because while M may be advanced *today*, ΔM can only be realized in the *future*— and the future always remains uncertain. Nonetheless, because this problem afflicts both options, it cannot determine the choice. Our entrepreneur has no option but to make those probabilistic calculations and then choose accordingly.

Ultimately the choice comes down to the basic form of the capitalist use of markets ($M \rightarrow C \rightarrow M'$); it becomes a question of what to buy— *capital goods* (MP and LP) or *financial securities*—and it can be framed in terms of return rates on those goods. Does the rate of return on the capital goods (expressed indirectly in the profit rate in that industry) exceed the interest rate paid on a bond?[7] If so, buy the capital goods; if not, buy the bond. Here we see why **interest rates are the metaphorical pulse of capitalism**: because as interest rates rise, the cost of borrowing to finance the purchase of capital goods goes up (reducing profit rates) at the same time as the rate of return on bonds also rises. Rising interest rates push our entrepreneur out of capital investment and toward safer, interest-bearing financial assets. Falling interest rates do just the opposite, since buying the financial asset becomes less attractive just as the cost to borrow to fund capitalist production falls (thus raising prospective returns to production). Interest rates therefore govern the flow of money and commodities in a capitalist economy since they regulate the advancement of money in capitalist production.[8]

The Bankers' Bank

What, then, governs interest rates? Who decides to "raise" or "lower" interest rates, how do they decide, and how do they implement such changes? Questions like these quickly spiral in complexity and go beyond the subject matter this book addresses regarding the fundamentals of studying capitalist economic forces and relations within a larger social order. But we can broach the question, make a few crucial clarifications of our analysis so far, and lay out some terms for future (advanced) investigation.

First, we must reiterate the underlying point: there is not one interest rate; there are always a variety of interest rates. Not all entrepreneurs (not everyone with available M) will face the same set of choices because they will face different prospective rates of return (on both capital goods and financial assets) and different interest rates. Second, even if we focus on one particular set of rates for one particular economic actor, we can never explain those rates as the result of a single (independent) variable. Interest rates are always overdetermined. Given this background, we can go on to identify one absolutely paramount, if not dominant, actor/institution: the central bank.

The central bank is not an omnipotent government agency that controls everything having to do with money. Indeed, we have already shown that most money creation in modern capitalist systems comes about through the actions of commercial banks, not central banks. Conspiracy theories about central banks and central bankers get us nowhere. Instead, the most incisive way to make sense out of the central bank and its role in a capitalist economy is to see that **the central bank is the bankers' bank.** As we have already shown, money is credit/debt; hence a modern money system is simply a complex ledger registering credits and debts. Here we just add one more wrinkle to that model by including another tier. As a consumer, my money assets take the form of credits held against my bank—that is, deposits in my account. For my bank, these same deposits are liabilities (they are what the bank owes me). The bank will also hold assets on their books in the form of loans owed by regular customers like me.

But in addition to credits/debts in relation to individual customers, the bank—in order to be a bank, that is, an institution that can be trusted financially—needs to have other resources, other credits than loans owed to it by individuals. The bank needs to have *reserves* in the form of higher-quality credits. For this, my bank (a regular commercial bank) needs its own bank, a place where its credits can be held.[9] The central bank (or better, a central banking system) plays this role: the central bank is the bankers' bank, and a regular commercial bank's reserves are nothing other than credits held in an account at the central bank. Thus, when a regular commercial bank needs to pay another commercial bank, it pays in central bank reserves. For example, if I write a check for $100 on My Bank and you cash it at Your Bank, this involves changes in four columns of the overall money ledger (all for the same $100 amount):

1. a debit to my checking account (reducing my credits and reducing My Bank's debt)
2. a credit to your checking account (increasing your credits and increasing Your Bank's debt)
3. a debit to My Bank's central bank reserve account (decreasing its credits)
4. a credit to Your Bank's central bank reserve account (increasing its credits)

As the so-called lender of last resort, as the bankers' bank, the central bank occupies the apex of the monetary system. This outline of the balance sheet of banks helps us to understand the principal tool that the central bank can wield to influence capitalist economics: the central bank determines the interest rate at which commercial banks can borrow central bank reserves. Because the structure of the banking system means that commercial banks need to hold credits at the central bank, and often need to borrow from the central bank, the central bank therefore holds a position of enormous structural power. Simply by setting and altering the central bank rate, this institution can effect changes in interest rates all across the economy. In overly simplified terms: commercial banks can only offer loans with rates higher than the central bank rate, and they can only pay interest rates (on savings accounts and CDs) that are lower than the central bank rate. When the central bank rates go up, the rates on mortgages and commercial lines of credit will soon rise; when rates go down, savings rates will soon decline (it should not surprise us that moves in the opposite direction—mortgage rate declines following a central bank rate reduction—often have a greater temporal lag).

We can now augment our conclusion from the previous section: if interest rates are the pulse of capitalism, and if (as we argued in the last chapter) entrepreneurs are the pacemakers, then the central bank is a cardiologist who can manipulate the pulse and alter the pacemaker's settings. Many other factors can contribute to small changes in the various interest rates, but no single entity has comparable influence on the broader movement of interest rates than the central bank. This means that the fundamental decision of entrepreneurs—to buy capital goods or to buy financial assets—will be massively shaped by the policy decisions and institutional choices of central bankers. When the central bank adjusts rates, it simultaneously, and dynamically, alters the decision matrix of entrepreneurs, and this, in turn, can have dramatic effects on the capitalist production process (and with it, economic activity all across the social order).

We have stated that the central bank is not omnipotent—no single actor can control all economic forces and relations—but we must emphasize two further points. Central banks and central bankers do, in fact, wield significant power, *and this power is very much political*. While there is a common discourse about both the "independence" of central banks and their commitment to follow technical rules, central bankers are appointed by legislative or executive political powers, and the rules they follow are ones that they themselves can reinterpret or even rewrite. For example, for many decades the US Federal Reserve declared its commitment to *balancing* economic growth with low inflation, which often meant preemptively raising interest rates (to prevent a rise in prices) in a way that slowed job growth, wage growth, and overall economic output. But in response to the global coronavirus pandemic, the Fed announced in August 2020 that it would prioritize economic growth and allow modest increases in inflation (above its 2 percent "target"). Central bankers today often appear to be centrists, resisting radical arguments from left and right, but the political center is still a site of important political power. Central banks are one of many crucial locations where political and economic forces intersect, often conflict, and frequently mutually enforce one another.

Moreover, central bank actions do more than influence the choices entrepreneurs make: they help to determine who will or will not be an entrepreneur. After all, the would-be entrepreneur who plows all of their money into stocks and bonds would wind up bypassing the capitalist mode of production entirely. At the limit, and as a thought experiment, we must see that if literally everyone with access to extra money chose to buy financial assets, the capitalist mode of production would grind to a halt and cease to circulate the very money and commodities that are the lifeblood of the system (the system that the speculator in financial assets depends on for appreciation). Economic activity in a capitalist social order is always determined by capitalist production: if the production process ceases, then the capitalist system *seizes*, and this leads to plummeting values across the board.

The Myth of Risk

This leads us to one final, essential point. Throughout the analysis of the preceding two chapters, we have tried to clarify the structural location of the entrepreneur within a capitalist mode of production, and also to map out the decision matrix that such an agent faces. By definition we have assumed our agent has available money (M), either in the form of savings (credits) or in the form of the availability of commercial loans. So at its core the driving question has been the choice of *how* the entrepreneur will spend that money.

This mode of analysis differs strikingly from the framing of the activity of "investors" that we often encounter in many domains across society today. In opinion columns, in the business press, and especially from pundits on twenty-four-hour news networks, one often sees the same question framed as the choice of *whether* the entrepreneur will "invest." We have already shown that often those references to "investment" are actually conflations of genuine capital investment with the purchasing of financial assets. Putting that aside, there is a more important issue at stake: the standard approach assumes that the entrepreneur has the option *not to spend* their available M, but instead simply to hold onto it. With this framing, the discussion usually turns to emphasize the importance, if not the necessity, of shaping social and political policy decisions so that we can *encourage* the entrepreneur to spend rather than hold her money. Finally, this discourse usually invokes the language of risk: the entrepreneur who chooses to invest is said to be *risking* her money by investing it and for that reason must therefore be rewarded for what is often depicted as brave action. The basic idea is that we want to make political decisions that reward investors for courageous risk-taking and not to discourage them because, it is presumed, entrepreneurs always have the option to take their money and go home (i.e., not to invest). The logic of this argument proves to be so ubiquitous that for many readers it might just sound like common sense.

However, the entire argument is premised on an untenable assumption, and it gives rise to a mythical construction of "risk" and risk-taking. The basic counterpoint is actually quite simple, as it rests on the understanding of money that we mapped out in Chapter 4 and then developed in more detail here. There is no such thing as a form of money with positive, intrinsic value. All money is credit/debt, which means all money is a social relation between creditor and debtor (to have money I need someone to owe me, a place to hold my credits), and such relations depend upon a wider monetary system that maintains the integrity of the ledger, which registers those credits and debts (in a sense, the money system is that ledger). This means that money is always future oriented. To "have" money is to hold credits that we hope will be good in the future. More than this, we hope that these credits will have at least as much, if not more, purchasing power in the future than they have today.

But this hope can never be ensured. The future validity of credits, the future purchasing power of money, can never be guaranteed. If I hold money in the stock of a company, the company can go bankrupt and the stock price can drop to zero. If I hold money in bonds, the issuer can default. If I hold money in a bank account, the bank can fail, wiping out my accounts. If I hold money in a government-insured bank account, the insurance fund can fail or the government can change policy. And any time I hold money in any form of "cash," I always have to worry about inflation, which over time can completely

erode the purchasing power of my money. All of this adds up to indicate decisively that there is no such thing as a riskless form of money;
there is no place to "hold" money that is sheltered from danger. All
money is at risk, always.

It is doubtless true that some forms of money, some investment
choices, are riskier than others. But none are risk free. Those who hold
large sums of money today are not doing society a favor by choosing to
invest rather than not invest their money; such actors have no choice
but to put their money somewhere, and wherever they put it there will
be a range of probabilities for returns and a degree of risk. Value in
capitalism is *always in motion, never static*. To understand capitalist economics we must therefore always maintain a sense of the **dynamic
forces and relations** that circulate value through the continuous exchange of money and commodities. Our final task in the book is to
bring to light some of the consistent forces, the tendencies, the gravitational fields that help to give a definite shape and form to capitalist
social orders.

Notes

1. Moreover, average profit rates attain rough parity across industries through
   capitalist competition. High profit rates in an industry encourage entrants,
   which reduces profit rates in the entered industry and raises them in the
   exited industry. We will elaborate on this point in Chapter 9.
2. In general terms, the larger the sum of M advanced, the larger the absolute
   quantity of ΔM realized. Entrepreneurs therefore face strong incentives to
   maximize the amount of M advanced for capitalist production and to min-
   imize other expenditures. One primary way to maximize the total amount
   M advanced is through borrowing leverage.
3. Seventy-one percent of the Earth's surface is ocean. If we exclude oceans and
   focus only on land, then approximately one-third is used for food production, while far less than 1 percent is used for all other forms of production.
4. Points 1 and 2 develop and conclude some of the analysis first raised
   back in Chapter 1 when we critically considered the "quantity theorem of
   money," which posits money as a commodity and asserts that changes in the
   "supply" of money will therefore lead to changes in the overall price level.
   The formula $(M * V) \uparrow \rightarrow (P * T) \uparrow$ (money supply times velocity causing

changes in price level times total transactions) tells us that an increase in "money supply" leads to higher price levels, that is, inflation. Our analysis in the text here utterly dissolves this theory by demonstrating that money is not a commodity (so it cannot have a "supply" in the same way as standard commodities) and interest rates are not its "price." The quantity theorem of money has endured for so long partially because its explanation of inflation is so parsimonious. The theory underlies claims such as this, which were commonplace in the early 2010s: "If the Fed keeps printing money, inflation is inevitable." Such claims have now proven to be false as the quantity of money in the economy has grown fourfold over the past decade, while inflation remained at historic lows. Inflation must be understood as primarily an *economic* phenomenon, not a *strictly monetary* phenomenon (contra Milton Friedman and other monetarists). If the prices of primary, necessary commodities go up (because of shortages, because of extremely high demand, etc.) then the prices of all goods and services will rise, and this is the very definition of inflation. And if prices go up, then the amount of money circulating in the economy will necessarily have to rise (simply in order for the same number of goods and services to be circulated at higher prices). There is also a related but *separate* question of "hyperinflation," which can occur with a loss in integrity of the monetary system itself, a fundamental failure of the money of account in which a social order's credits and debts are denominated.

5. Most economists try to work their way around this problem by arguing that different interest rates are simply different measures of the same underlying variable. Rates change (they argue) because of varying *term* lengths and varying *risk* factors, but underneath there is still a certain law of one interest rate in the same way there is a law of one price. This is a poor patch on a weak theory.

6. Prior to the financial crisis, the London Interbank Offered Rate (LIBOR) was an attempt to create a stable "singular" interest rate, but the crisis revealed that the rate itself had been actively manipulated by bankers. Since the crisis financial authorities have been considering pushing for a shift to the Secured Overnight Financing Rate (SOFR) because it is meant to be more directly measurable and not manipulable. Unfortunately for this project, SOFR is exactly the rate that "blew up" in late 2019: a rate that was meant to stay in a "normal" range of about 2.00–2.25 percent spiked to as much as 10 percent in certain instances.

7. This is effectively a measure of the overall productivity of capitalist production (its capacity to generate surplus value), but to clarify the importance of this factor in terms of entrepreneurial decision-making, it can be stylized as

the difference between the interest rate (as a direct return on money) and what John Maynard Keynes called the "marginal efficiency of capital" (as the return to capital goods). It illuminatingly boils down to this: do I buy a crane or a bond?

8. Relatedly, interest rates also help to determine the market value of capital goods since the prices of those goods are partially determined by the relation between their prospective return (when used in the production process) and the ruling rate of interest. To take a rough example, assume a robot contributes $1,000 of net value to a production process with a one-year period of production. If the interest rate charged to robot-buying entrepreneurs is 5 percent, then the market price of the robot should be $20,000, because a 5 percent annual percentage rate on $20,000 yields $1,000, and it would therefore make little sense to buy the robot at a higher price (or sell it at a lower price). Notice what happens when the interest rate drops to 2 percent: the market price of the robot should rise to $50,000. This example is oversimplified (and surely the robot's price would not jump that high) precisely because it assumes too many other variables remain static when the interest rate changes, but it helps to illustrate the crucial point that changes in interest rates affect the values of commodities all across the economy.

9. Actual currency—coins and notes—is another form of bank assets, though the amount held by most modern banks is tiny. Nonetheless, currency is really just another form of central bank reserves because coins and paper notes are the circulating debt of the national government (and the central bank is a governmental institution). Regardless of whether it takes the form of a $20 bill in a vault, or the form of a $20 credit in a Federal Reserve bank account, that $20 is a commercial bank asset, a credit held against the government. The one key difference is that currency can circulate publicly whereas central bank reserves cannot: I can get the $20 note out of the ATM as a draw on my checking account, but I cannot withdraw central bank reserves from that account. Only commercial banks, not individuals, get accounts with the central bank. The recent suggestion to create central bank digital wallets and make them available directly to all citizens would thus be a radical monetary invention, as it could potentially allow individuals to bypass commercial bank accounts.

9

The Rules of Capitalism

The Anti-Robinsonade

In a way we have returned to where we began in Chapter 1, as only now do we find ourselves in a position to make broader, generalizing claims about capitalist economic forces and relations. As we noted at the beginning, many texts in the history of economic thought start with a highly stylized account of "economic man" in a putative "state of nature." This skeletal structure makes it possible for those works to make strong proclamations about "fundamental" economic forces; the idea is that in their very nature human beings are economic creatures who naturally exchange, barter, buy, sell, and seek profit. We showed decisively in Chapter 1, and then underscored the point repeatedly throughout the book, that there is no such thing as a "state of nature" other than as a literary device created by human beings already living in an intricate and complicated capitalist (or emerging capitalist) social order. In this book we have therefore repeatedly eschewed the Robinsonade.

In fact, we might describe our method as mobilizing an anti-Robinsonade: rather than assume key features of humans as transhistorical truths, and then use those features as primary particles from which to build up an account of economics and the economy, we have instead consistently refused to assume anything about human beings as "natural" or given. Instead we started with concrete history itself, with the development and first emergence of a capitalist mode of production as a unique, unexpected, and certainly not predictable historical event. By situating economics as *economicus* in historical context, we made it possible to grasp a capitalist social order as distinct and peculiar in many important ways. From this starting point we could then analyze principal capitalist elements or relations (money, commodities, profits) and study the actions and choices of principal economic

Capitalist Economics. Samuel A. Chambers, Oxford University Press. © Oxford University Press 2022.
DOI: 10.1093/oso/9780197556887.003.0010

actors (entrepreneurs, workers, bankers). Only after accomplishing all of that do we have a clear enough picture of a capitalist social order to ask the more general question: **What are the rules of capitalism?**

Importantly, this question is not about the static nature of human beings, or the fixed essence of capitalism, but rather about the general tendencies, the propensities found in a capitalist social order. While the cliché "rules are made to be broken" probably overstates the case, it suggests a kernel of truth: rules are not inviolable—indeed, they are violated all the time, and often only emerge to us clearly *as rules* in the instances of their violation.[1] Hence our final project here is not to establish transhistorical laws of capitalism or to make predictions about its inevitable progress or decline. Rather, the plan in this final chapter is to look at a capitalist social order as a complex and dynamic whole and to try to pull out key features of it that function as general rules of capitalism. To repeat, these rules can be and often are broken. But more than this, the rules can be modified, altered, and even partially rewritten; this is especially the case because the economic forces that give rise to these rules (the general tendencies or proclivities of a capitalist mode of production) always operate within the context of social, legal, cultural, and political rules. One rule may occasionally or even consistently clash with another rule, and nothing can guarantee in advance how such a conflict will be dealt with—or what the ultimate result will be. Thus, this account of the rules guarantees nothing: it will not provide you with a crystal ball to tell the future of capitalism, nor help you to beat the stock market.

Nevertheless, **capitalism does have rules** in the form of often very powerful forces and tendencies; these cannot be ignored or dismissed. We cannot pretend such rules don't exist or that they can be merely overwritten by other ethical or political principles; both defenders and critics of capitalism who assume otherwise do so at their peril. For this reason, it is imperative that any attempt to understand capitalist economics (the central aim of this book) also includes an effort to map out the rules of capitalism and to understand how, to what end, and within what constraints they function. We therefore conclude the book with just such a project, which takes the very simple form of listing the rules.

Rule 1: Money Must Beget More Money

The primary rule of capitalism is nothing other than the cardinal expression of the driving economic force within a capitalist social order. To capture this core capitalist imperative, we can return to our code for the capitalist mode of production:

$$M \to C...P...C' \to M'$$

This code describes a process by which a starting sum of economic value moves through a system of transformations in order to arrive at an end point where it reappears as a larger sum of economic value. These "transformations" are literal: the value first appears as money (M), then as commodities (MP and LP), then as a wholly different set of commodities (finished goods, C'), and finally again as more money (M'). The first rule of capitalism is that it is a system in which value changes forms and, as it does so, always attempts to grow into more value. Viewed from a wide enough depth of field, it even appears as if this quantum of value is itself the primary *agent* of the system (value seems to grow all on its own). The first rule of capitalism is that value grows into more value.

In more concrete terms, we can say that capitalism requires that production in a society be organized and executed according to the capitalist use of the market, $M \to M'$. In its capitalist use, the market becomes the site for the realization of surplus value, the location for the attainment of profit. Because capitalism is fundamentally the rearrangement of production according to this market principle, the market becomes a *central constraining force* across the entire social order. Put differently, the first rule of capitalism is to **obey market principles**—above all the principle of maximizing profit.

This unique use of the market requires that one advance money (M) so as to produce surplus money (ΔM) and arrive at more total money (M'). Under capitalism, money is of course used for many purposes, and most people in society may never have occasion to use money to beget more money. Nevertheless, under capitalism, the meaning of money par excellence is to be found in its use to initiate and carry out capitalist production. While money will always have many uses within a capitalist social order, **if money ceases to be used to beget more money, the social order ceases to be capitalist**. Hence this rule is the prime directive of capitalism.

While all the rules of capitalism may be violated in some sense, this first rule proves, in a technical sense, unbreakable. Of course it is quite possible to rearrange production processes such that they are no longer driven by market imperatives, but at the moment this occurs our social order ceases to be capitalist. So to break this first rule, this prime directive, is to break capitalism itself.

Rule 1a: Money Is the Means of Survival

This rule is nothing more than a direct corollary of the first (hence the numbering) but its broad-scale significance justifies the separate entry. Because the capitalist use of the market governs and constrains social production, capitalist social orders are marked by both the *ubiquity* and *necessity* of money. Under capitalism, life's basic necessities are produced for profitable sale on the market, and this means that in order to obtain even the most minimal goods and services required to live, one must first attain money. Aside from exceptional and highly limited circumstances, food, clothing, and shelter cannot be produced directly or acquired outside the market; they must be purchased on the market, with money. This means that under capitalism the primary requirement for survival becomes money itself; you cannot live without it.

Rule 1 applies at the most general level of description of a capitalist social order. Rule 1a applies at both that general level and also across and throughout the entire structure of society. It reaches everywhere, and hence it applies to everyone: producers, workers, traders, the rich, the poor—everyone needs money to live. We can spotlight the importance of this rule by thinking about it in comparison to other social orders: in all social orders that we know of (across history), human beings have always needed certain basic goods to survive. Without some form, no matter how limited, of clothing and shelter, humans will soon perish. Without food and water, they will die even more quickly. This makes these primary goods requirements of survival in all known social orders. **Only under capitalism does money take on a status similar to food and water;** only within a social order structured by the capitalist mode of production does money become so essential and precious.

Rules 1 and 1a are the most general rules of capitalism. They are ubiquitous; they apply at all levels, in all places, and to all individuals within society. *Within capitalism, they are universal*; this means that while they remain historically contingent, they operate generally across a capitalist social order. As we move on to adumbrate the remaining rules, we will see that some of them apply most directly to certain actors within capitalism; the specific force of particular rules registers most decisively at certain structural locations within a capitalist social order. For example, Rule 2 centers on the market, so it immediately impacts buyers and sellers of goods, while Rules 3 and 4 apply particularly to producers, entrepreneurs, and enterprise managers. Whether or not a particular rule will apply to a particular individual depends directly on that individual's location within the capitalist mode of production— worker or capitalist, producer of capitalist goods or member of the financial services industry, and so on. Nonetheless, all the rules affect everyone indirectly: if you are a banker then you must follow (or bear the consequences of not following) any rules that apply directly to bankers, but if you are not a banker, you should still be very interested in learning any rules that apply to bankers, because those rules will also affect you—indirectly yet powerfully—if and when you need a loan.[2]

Rule 2: Markets Regulate Prices

Under this rule we find a number of sub-rules that make up a large bulk of the principles of the neoclassical paradigm of economics. As our delineation of them here will indicate, these principles are not false, but they are narrowly circumscribed, and they too are only rules of *capitalism*, not universal laws. The main rule is simple: the basic principles of supply and demand will largely, *but not entirely*, determine market prices.

In turn, the principles of supply and demand are nothing more than a simple pair of causal relations, with ceteris paribus conditions. We can state them succinctly in the language we described in Chapter 1, where supply and demand are the independent variables and price is the dependent variable. Ceteris paribus:

2a. Supply of a commodity is inversely (negatively) related to price, $S_c \uparrow \rightarrow P_c \downarrow$

2b. Demand for a commodity is directly (positively) related to price, $D_c \uparrow \rightarrow P_c \uparrow$

In simpler language: excess demand drives prices up, while excess supply drives prices down, and vice versa. All of us who live under capitalism are so familiar with these rules that they sound like common sense.[3] In November, the newly released gaming console will be expensive because holiday demand is high and supply is constrained, while at exactly the same time the piling-up inventory of current-model-year cars will make particular cars available for bargain discounts.

There is a bigger point to underscore about the force of the market in setting prices through the balancing of supply and demand: overall the market determines prices such that both buyers and sellers of commodities find themselves in the position of "price takers." The price is the price; it is *given* by the market and cannot be altered directly in the market by those engaged in exchange transactions. There is no haggling, either on Amazon or at the grocery store: there is only one price. Of course, there are domains of a capitalist order where price is negotiable. However, this exception proves the rule, (1) because even the haggling is meant to revolve around the gravitational pull of a single market price, and (2) because these domains, like craigslist, exist not at the center but at the margins of a capitalist market. Indeed, haggling over price is often thought to reveal the truth of market forces, in that the auction can be understood as a pure form of market negotiation. Note also that among the group of buyers who are price takers, we also find *producers*, who must make their plans for production based on given market pricing. In this way, Rule 2 has knock-on effects on many other rules, especially Rule 3.

Rule 3: Producers Must Produce
Profitable Commodities[4]

In some ways this rule could be thought of as the most important rule of capitalism: it proves central to our definition of capitalism as a social order centered on a capitalist mode of production. This rule expresses the basic insight that nothing can be produced under capitalism unless it realizes a profit. For those involved in, or considering taking up, the production of capitalist commodities (whether they be entrepreneurs, managers of enterprises, or inventors) a good idea is not necessarily a good capitalist idea, because a production process can only be planned and initiated if its completion holds the viable promise of the realization of positive net revenue, of profits. Wide-eyed would-be entrepreneurs sometimes forget this rule in their rush to "change the world," but bankers and venture capitalists always remind them quickly, since the failure to make this rule primary is the number one reason why this latter group rejects requests for capital funding.

At the first level, this rule is simple to follow: the plan to produce a capitalist commodity must include a budget, and in that budget total costs must be less than total gross revenue—expected M' must exceed the total cost of C. And when it comes to the expected value of the sales of C', producers must keep Rule 2 in mind: once their production process is complete and they offer the finished good on the market, they will find themselves in the position of price-takers. If the market price is too low to realize ΔM, then the business will fail for lack of profits (or just as likely, it will never get funded in the first place).

Furthermore, almost more significant than the basic rule are two subsidiary rules, which combine insights from Rule 2 and Rule 3:

3a. Prices of your commodity will always tend to be falling.
    Competition among firms *in your industry* will always tend to drive prices down, because every firm is trying to sell as much of their finished goods as possible and because higher prices will encourage new firms to enter the market (and undercut current prices).

3b. Profit rates in your industry will always tend to be falling.
Competition among firms *across industries* means that if profit
rates in your particular industry are high, entrepreneurs will re-
direct M toward production in your industry, thereby lowering
profit rates via the same mechanism as 3a (competition). *See also
Rule 5.*

When capitalism is misunderstood as nothing more than market exchange, it then gets misdescribed as strictly an "opportunity" to trade
in a market to achieve the mutual satisfaction of market participants'
needs and wants. With Rule 3 we see the power of the market as a
constraining, regulating, and disciplining force on the capitalist producer, who violates its rules to his detriment.

Rule 4: Technological Change and "Innovation" are
Required (Not Optional)

This rule connects to and extends the previous one. Both apply most
forcefully to the producer, but this one has dramatic implications that
reverberate all across a capitalist social order. The best viewpoint for
grasping this rule can be found if we place ourselves in the office chair
of the capitalist enterprise manager as he views the spreadsheet showing
total costs, total revenue, and most importantly, net revenue (functional
profits). We know that our overriding goal is to increase net revenue,
and this can only be done by decreasing costs or increasing revenue.
Moreover, the previous two rules indicate how constrained we are by capitalist economic forces in any efforts to achieve the latter; we are price-
takers working with fixed demand for our firm's output. In the short term,
and as a manager (who cannot authorize massive initiatives for new or
extended production processes) it will always prove difficult to increase
gross revenues meaningfully. Our focus thus turns to costs: How can we
drive down costs quickly so that net revenue increases?

As we know, our costs are C, made up of MP and LP. We buy our
means of production on the market, so the prices there are given to us
and cannot be meaningfully changed.[5] This leads us to look at LP, the
wages we pay workers. If possible, we could pay workers less or hold

down any raises. We might also consider ways to extend their total work time without increasing pay: with salaried workers this is easy (since pay is fixed); with hourly workers it can be trickier, and there are limits (legal, physical, etc.). All of these, however, prove to be minor adjustments, so let's assume for the sake of this example that we have already done everything possible in these areas and that we think we are getting as much time out of workers as possible. We must implement a bigger change that can significantly affect the bottom line.

What if we could alter the very structure of production such that each labor-hour led to a greater output of our produced commodity? This would appear to be a game changer as we could produce the same output for less, thereby immediately increasing net revenue (i.e., profits). What we are describing here is an increase in the overall **productivity** of our production process: we are producing more total output (measured in terms of quantities of commodities) per labor-hour.[6]

The question then becomes: How do we achieve these productivity increases? Assume you are the manager of a busy, high-volume coffee shop and your goal is to increase productivity: you want to sell (at least) the same number of scones and cappuccinos while reducing the weekly labor-hours. You might achieve limited success by changing the way you order and manage the production process. Perhaps you can place only three employees on the floor, rather than four, by having one person rotate from helping out on the espresso bar to expediting orders for the cashier. But this might only work at slower times, and you could find it almost impossible to create a weekly schedule that doesn't leave you understaffed at certain hours. The better, more radical solution would be to buy a new automated espresso machine. With the time saved by automating grinding and pulling of espresso shots, you could completely eliminate the need for a second person to work the espresso bar. Now you can drop all of your shifts down to three people, boosting productivity across the board and saving dramatically on labor costs.

The above logical example gives concrete expression to the basic rule: if you are an enterprise owner or manager, **you must *constantly* find new and better ways to increase productivity** and thereby reduce labor costs. Under capitalism, each and every enterprise owner has an extremely strong incentive to search for technological improvements in the production process. Collectively, we find throughout history that the capitalist mode of production has consistently and repeatedly increased productivity through technological change and improvements. As Ellen Meiksins Wood puts it, "capitalism is a system *uniquely driven to improve the productivity of labour* by technical means" (Wood 2002: 3, emphasis added).

This has numerous, profound implications: it means that technological innovation is itself an internal rule of capitalism. Enterprise owners *must* implement technological change in order to remain competitive. Technological development does not occur automatically, autonomously, or because of independently driven scientific curiosity. Rather, **the capitalist mode of production drives technology**. Moreover, even "innovation" is inherent to the system. "Innovation" is not external to the system, something that comes only from the minds of unique geniuses. Rather, capitalism requires innovation of all producers; it forces entrepreneurs to "innovate." Capitalists have no choice but to increase productivity: therefore technological transformations are *endogenous* to the capitalist mode of production.

This rule reveals that many of the elements for which capitalism is most celebrated are not side effects or complements to the system but actually inherent forces within the capitalist mode of production, and they are derivative of the primary drive of value augmentation. Technology and innovation prove instrumental to capitalism: they are forces produced and harnessed for capital's own primary purpose— for the use of money to generate more money. This means we cannot easily disconnect technological developments from the capitalist drive toward profit maximization. Moreover, and much more portentously, it means that capitalist production creates its own counter-forces.

Rule 5: Crisis Is Unavoidable

Every production process is subject to various dangers, and none can avoid the possibility of crisis. This rule, however, expresses yet one last way in which a capitalist mode of production is unique: capitalism is the only system that produces its own production crises as an internal element of its system of production. Crisis is unavoidable under capitalism because *capitalism creates its own crises.*

To unpack this claim, let's look at a critical test case: a crisis in food production that leads to a societal "hunger problem" (i.e., large numbers of people who lack adequate amounts of food). Under precapitalist modes of production food shortages were common, and they almost always led to societal hunger problems. Typically such shortages had natural causes: famines were caused by drought or other forms of crop failure; people went hungry because there literally was not enough food to eat. In contrast, under capitalism the hunger problem exists (and persists) even in the absence of drought or crop failure. Recent data from the United States present the case starkly: US agriculture has a total annual output of approximately 4,000 calories per person per day, yet in 2015 more than 17 million US households were "food insecure." This means, according to the US Department of Agriculture, that at some point in the year, some members of that household did not have enough access to food to live an "active, healthy" life. A capitalist mode of production can therefore starkly illustrate the "paradox of poverty in the midst of plenty," as students of capitalist economics have long noted.

Yet the paradox runs deeper than the mere fact that a society can contain both wealth and poverty. Under previous modes of production the problem was always a *shortage*: of food, of basic commodities, of necessary production goods, and so on. Of course, a capitalist social order can fall victim to exogenous forces just like any other. War, drought, and floods can afflict *any* social order, and capitalist social orders can thus experience shortages as well. But **capitalism creates its own crises**, even in the absence of these exogenous shocks, and, uniquely, capitalism produces a *crisis of surplus*. That is, the capitalist mode of production is the only one in which a surplus of commodities constitutes its own peculiar problem.

Excess surplus, and with it the massive *destruction of value*, can occur whenever the overall demand for commodities falls well short of the amount produced. This means that unemployment can occur any time that the production plans of entrepreneurs (given their expectations about future demand) lead them to offer wage contracts to fewer than those willing to work. Whenever one of those mechanisms (falling demand or falling production) leads to and is reinforced by the other, we find ourselves in a full-blown crisis of capitalism: unsold commodities pile up, productive machines stand idle, and workers cannot find jobs. Under capitalism we can have an excess of goods and also, *at the very same time*, an excess of individuals willing to work for a wage.

This inherent potential and tendency toward crisis can be described in two different ways. First, we outline the overall possibility of crisis by working at the level of our general code for capitalist production. Then we detail the central mechanism by which this potential will be repeatedly (cyclically) experienced as an actual crisis. To start with the structural possibility, let's look one final time at our code for capitalist production:

$$M \rightarrow C...P...C' \rightarrow M'$$

There are two points of weakness:

1. $C' \rightarrow M'$

    The entrepreneur lacks control over this process. No matter how much he plans, calculates, and projects, at the end of the day— that is, at the end of the production process—he must subject himself to the forces of the market. He must offer his finished good (C') for sale and hope that the value contained in it (ΔC) can be realized (as ΔM). If no one is willing to buy C' at the market price that our entrepreneur predicted prior to his initiating production, then the entire process may (and likely will) result not in the realization of surplus value, but in an overall loss of value.[7]

2. *The initial sum of M*

    As we detailed in Chapter 8, the amount of M initially advanced by the capitalist depends on his consideration of the trade-offs involved in either buying capital goods or purchasing financial assets, as well as on his own expectations about future demand. If those calculations guide the entrepreneur to advance less M to start the next production process than was advanced in the previous process—that is, to cut back on capital investment—this can lead to more unemployment and, in turn, even further decreases in demand. From here a downward spiral sets in.

This gives us a wide-range sense of the weak links in the chain of value that constitutes the capitalist mode of production. Now we need to describe one of the fundamental mechanisms that consistently pushes the system toward crisis. To capture this dimension of the system, let's return to our adopted viewpoint in Rule 4: we are the manager of a capitalist enterprise, attempting to maximize profits. Accordingly, we strive to increase labor productivity through technological innovation. Here we need to follow through on our earlier example by considering not just our coffee shop but the entire coffee shop sector or "industry." When we do so, we find that our individual rationality to increase profits by increasing productivity has paradoxical and destabilizing effects when applied to the sector as a whole.

Earlier we just assumed that with greater productivity we would reap larger profits, but this was a bad assumption because it ignored the basic principle of competition among capitalist firms. Other entrepreneurs will quickly take note of both our new technology and our increased profits, and this will give them incentives to (1) enter the coffee-shop business, (2) replicate our technological mix, and (3) undercut us by offering lower prices (or extra perks). If standard profit rates in our sector are 10 percent and our technological change generated a profit rate of 15 percent, this rate will not last for more than a few economic periods. High profit rates will lead directly to increased competition and lowered prices. In order to keep up with the new entrants to the market (or changes made by our long-standing competitors), we will have to lower our prices as well, with the end result that profit rates will stabilize at their previous level. Our supposed great idea only generated increased profits for a temporary period: the end result is not a stable increase to long-term profits but an overall decrease of the price of the commodities we sell. Morcover, because the profit rate is itself a percentage of the production costs, by driving down our production costs (through the increase in productivity) we have simultaneously pushed down our absolute profits.

Summarizing and generalizing: from the perspective of the individual capitalist, increasing productivity appears to lead to increased profits. But the effect is only temporary because each productivity increase introduced by one capitalist is soon copied by all capitalists in that industry, with the result that the extra profit disappears. What is left behind? Lower prices and lower total profits (the generation of less overall surplus value). The drive by individual entrepreneurs to increase individual profit actually leads to an overall decrease in prices, and with it, total available profits (surplus value) for all entrepreneurs as a class. Ultimately this means that in their effort to compete with one another and try to maximize profits, individual entrepreneurs create an overall structural situation in which profits are falling. This point can also be expressed in the language of the "marginal efficiency of capital" from the last chapter: capital goods generate more return the scarcer they are. As capital accumulates, after many cycles of $M \rightarrow M'$, we reach a point where capital goods can no longer generate reasonable returns, and the entrepreneur will thus reduce capital investment.

And at this point we can link the two pieces together, because falling profit rates will change the entrepreneur's calculus at the start of each production period: as profit rates fall, it becomes more likely that the smart choice will be *not* to buy capital goods but instead to buy financial assets—a choice that puts us back on the downward spiral. Regardless of how we describe the process, we observe the same overriding rule: **a capitalist mode of production tends toward crisis.** This conclusion requires two important clarifications.

First, to say that "crisis is unavoidable" is not to say that "collapse" is inevitable. Since the dawn of capitalism, critics have been proclaiming its imminent demise—and none of their predictions have come true. Nothing in the capitalist mode of production guarantees that it will "overcome itself"; that is, nothing in the capitalist system inherently leads to its transformation to a different mode of production. As we saw briefly in the transition from feudalism to capitalism, a full-scale revolution in the mode of production does not come about strictly because of economic forces alone; rather, such a revolution requires a whole host of other social, cultural, and political transformations. Crisis must not be confused with collapse (or transformation); collapse is only one possible result of dealing with the crisis, and there is an infinite variety of ways to respond to crises—some that significantly ameliorate the effects of the crisis, and some that exacerbate them.

Second, a capitalist crisis is always a crisis of value, and nothing does more to create conditions for capitalist growth than the destruction of value. In a full-blown crisis, values plummet. Factories sit unused, and inventories sit unsold: prior to the crisis these all had high book values that reflected the contribution of value to production and their expected realization of value after sale, but during the crisis the capitalist has no choice but to "write them down" or "write them off," phrases that indicate precisely that value is simply reduced (often dramatically) by changing numbers on a spreadsheet. As companies report losses the value of their stock plummets. Bond issuers default. Individual firms go bankrupt, and overall production is severely curtailed. Last but not least, unemployed workers no longer receive paychecks. Money is destroyed all across the board, and in many cases commodities are destroyed too (as piled-up inventories are burned or buried or otherwise disposed of). Capitalist crises can be more or less destructive to the individual lives of workers and entrepreneurs, depending on the nature of the industry these individuals are in and depending even more significantly on the social policies, economic mechanisms, and other political systems in place to deal with a crisis. But regardless of the extent of the destruction of social wealth and individual suffering, **capitalist crises always destroy value.**[8]

But precisely this destruction of value makes renewed capital growth possible. As Michael Heinrich puts the point, capitalist crises are very much "productive" when viewed from the system level. The destruction of capital (in the form of the offline factories and bankrupt firms) and the reduction of wages created by high unemployment lead to ideal conditions for renewed capital investment. Capital goods have been made scarce by the crisis, and labor-power has been made cheap. Once the slump is over, capitalist production will then yield a much higher return. At the bottom, opportunities abound to reap huge profits.

Overall, from the perspective of the capital relation, a crisis is the greatest tonic. This point ties back to our previous one, since it shows us that if a capitalist social order survives a crisis even minimally intact, then it will easily avoid collapse—because the crisis itself produces the conditions for renewed (relative) prosperity. **Each capitalist crisis thus offers the possibility of revolutionary transformation** (the creation of a new mode of production) **while also providing a path toward the preservation of the capitalist social order**—with its in-built tendency toward the next crisis.

Notes

1. Think particularly about social rules—norms, mores, etiquette—that you had no idea existed until someone pointed out that you had violated them.
2. This example is merely a heuristic because this list contains no rules applying specifically to bankers. Still, it would be easy to formulate the most important such rule: you must lend at rates higher than those at which you borrow. Thus the main set of rules enumerated here easily gives rise to a long list of derivative rules or corollaries.
3. Nevertheless, even in the realm of supply and demand, the rules can be broken. The best recent counterexample can be found in the case of literally the single most important commodity in the global economy today, the Apple iPhone. (Note that oil, or even clean air, might be the most important *resource* in the world, but the iPhone is the most important commodity for the largest and most profitable corporation, so it is the most important *commodity*.) From its release in 2007, demand for the iPhone rose consistently, and in 2015 Apple sold a record 231 million iPhones. From 2015 through the end of the decade, however, demand for iPhones dropped. What happened to the price of iPhones after 2015? *It went up a lot.* In 2015 the base model of Apple's newest phone (iPhone 6) sold for $549; in 2018 the base model of Apple's newest phone (iPhone XS) sold for $999. With this dramatic increase in prices, Apple managed to bring in more total revenue, more realized value (M') through iPhone sales, despite selling fewer iPhones. (At this time Apple switched from reporting numbers of iPhones sold to reporting total revenue, underscoring the point that realized value, M', is what matters most.) There is no simple explanation for this feat, but to offer such an explanation would require accounting for other forces in the social order (political, cultural) and recognizing plainly that the market force of supply and demand is not inviolable.
4. At this point in the book it should go without saying that whether a commodity is profitable depends not on anything intrinsic to the commodity as such (there is no "profitable" *type* of commodity) but on the nature of that commodity's production process in relation to the overall capitalist social order.

5. Of course we can try to reduce costs by choosing new suppliers, buying in bulk, and so on. But our competitors will always be doing the same, so unless we can gain *monopsony power* (the power that allows *us* to set the price our suppliers charge because we are the dominant or only purchaser of their production commodity), these savings will have no impact on our bottom line.

6. "Productivity" is often a confused and confusing term, so two clarifications are in order. First, the statistic is typically reported as "*labor* productivity" because labor-hours are the denominator. But our analysis here emphasizes that productivity reflects changes in the overall efficiency of a production process, which includes *both* labor-power and capital goods. Second, all national empirical measures of productivity are based on measures of output in money terms, but as we will see in the text that follows, this can be deceiving. Thus, our conceptualization centers on concrete output (i.e., the *number* of commodities produced) per labor-hour in a given industry.

7. This happens every day to individual enterprises, and sometimes even to wider sectors. Going out of business is a normal part of capitalist practices. The point in the text is therefore not to equate the bankruptcy of one enterprise with a failure in the system, but to identify a critical juncture in the process (the realization of value, $C' \rightarrow M'$). If something leads to a lack of realization for a wide swath of enterprises across the social order, then the problem will prove contagious and crisis will result.

8. Economists today have grown fond of measuring the difference between actual national economic output (measured in gross domestic product, GDP) and expected, potential, or counterfactual GDP, which is basically the GDP that would have been were it not for the depressed economic output of the recession. This measured difference is one way of getting at the destruction of value we are describing.

Sources and Further Reading

Sources

Most academic works are so deeply embedded in earlier scholarly debates, so thoroughly enmeshed in the extant academic literature, that it can prove almost impossible for a general reader to see through the thicket of citations and find the actual point of the text. The multiplicity of positions, arguments, and viewpoints can also prove disorienting for most readers, who may wonder exactly *where* they are on the map, and who might have no idea where to go after finishing the text before them. At the other extreme, most formal textbooks present their material as if it were sheer, unadorned, and objective fact, as if the claims of the textbook were beyond reproach, simply accepted as truth by all members of the academic discipline. As such, most textbooks cite very little of the previous work on which their own arguments are based; indeed, within many disciplines of the social and natural sciences, one point of textbooks seems to be to make it possible for students to *forget* (or never need to learn) anything about the work that came before the moment in time when the textbook itself was written. The textbook genre also strongly suggests that the only logical path to follow after finishing the book and completing the course in which it was assigned is to move on to the next course in the sequence (from intro to intermediate, or intermediate to advanced).

As neither a standard academic work nor a typical textbook, this book has a distinct and significant relationship to the sources from which it draws. On the one hand, the book itself explicitly cites very few works or authors directly: aside from an endnote here or there, the body of the text aims to establish a direct line of communication with the reader and therefore removes the impediments that would be created by constant and lengthy strings of parenthetical cites or piles of footnotes that end up taking over the majority of each page of the book. The exclusion from the main text of disciplinary debates or even citation of sources should be seen as a very conscious choice to achieve the intended aim of offering an *introduction* to political economy that can help explain capitalist economics in a short, readable book. However, on the other hand, there can and must be no pretense that the claims, descriptions, analyses, explanations, and arguments of this book add up to the received and agreed-upon wisdom of any academic discipline. Nor should it be presumed that the material presented here is merely an amalgamation of what has been said before. Quite to the contrary, none of the sources that this book draws from would be likely to agree with everything contained herein, and many authors might not recognize the use to which their ideas have been put. The assembled view presented in this book is unique—and belongs uniquely to the author.

Yet that view would not have been possible without so much work done by so many others. This section of the book therefore has two aims:

1. To **acknowledge** an incredibly broad range of sources without which the ideas of this book would never have been possible, and on which much of the overall architecture of *Capitalist Economics* is based.
2. To **direct** engaged and curious readers toward key (and, ideally, accessible) texts that ground and/or expand central tenets of this book.

As was noted in the preface, while this book is introductory it does not introduce readers to an extant academic field. For just that reason, the sources the book draws from prove extremely broad and interdisciplinary. The following are just some of the disciplines that this text calls on: anthropology, economics, English, history, philosophy, political and social theory, political science, and sociology. Given that the book cuts across so many academic fields, trying to provide a direct or chronological listing of sources would only confuse matters further—because as we move *forward* in time we would be moving *back and forth* across disciplines, in a manner that would appear to lack any coherent principle. Therefore, rather than presenting a crude list of every author and text, the sources and recommendations for further reading will be presented in rough accordance with the section and chapter structure of the book itself.

Prior to any particular sources, before any specific authors or arguments, the foundation of this book— its central ideas and primary approaches—rests on a long tradition of social and political theory. First, central conceptions of society as a social order can be traced back to nineteenth-century European thinkers such as Max Weber and Émile Durkheim—ideas that were reconceived in crucial ways by late twentieth-century French writers such as Louis Althusser, Michel Foucault, and Jacques Rancière. From the former we derive the notion that a social order has a kind of structural integrity to it, and that structure is arranged hierarchically (with vertical relations of power). From the latter we see that such a structure is not rigid: the various elements of the order (social, economic, cultural, political) are neither fixed in place nor hermetically sealed off from one another. Next, contemporary political theorists such as Wendy Brown and Bonnie Honig have developed crucial arguments about power and democratic political subjectivity—arguments rooted in this earlier tradition that also transform it. Finally, contemporary political scientists such as James Scott or Timothy Mitchell do not build directly from these foundations, but they do present arguments that resonate with or reflect them, all while exploring concrete political examples. All of these ideas form the primordial soup out of which the very approach to understanding a social order within history takes shape in this book.

The story told in the preface of the book—a story about the making of textbooks, a tale designed to show the *essentially political* nature of economics—comes from Zachary Carter's biography of Keynes. Speaking quite generally, the late nineteenth and early twentieth century mark the most important, most *formative* historical period for the central arguments of this book. We see in that period both the development of ideas in the field of economics and the occurrence of certain events in the world that help us to understand capitalist economics today. In an important way, history proves primary for this book—both the history of economic thought and the history of the emergence and transformation of capitalist economics.

The centrality of history can be clearly seen in Part I, which explicitly locates economic forces and relations within history. General sources for these arguments range widely across anthropology, economics, and history itself (as a discipline), but there are a few specific inspirations for the methodological approach taken here. It draws both from the genealogical approach of Friedrich Nietzsche and Michel Foucault and also, perhaps surprisingly, from a particular reading of G. W. F. Hegel's account of a dialectical logic. That combination may seem surprising because Nietzsche and Foucault were both vituperative critics of Hegel, but Marx's reading of Hegel in his "1857 Introduction" sets the stage for precisely the historical account of economic forces that this book mobilizes. In an earlier book, *Bearing Society in Mind*, I developed this approach more fully, but it is also one both implemented and articulated by thinkers such as Stuart Hall or Ellen Meiksins Wood.

The specific thesis that the origins of capitalism, as a unique mode of production, lay in the revolution in food production in the sixteenth-century English countryside was first sketched by Robert Brenner, then further advanced and reformulated by Wood (particularly in her aptly titled book *The Origin of Capitalism*, first published in 1999). This important scholarship has been very productively complicated by the recent, deeply insightful work of Jairus Banaji. Banaji traces the global forces of capital that circulate in a commercial capitalism that predates *by many centuries* the transition of any particular society to a capitalist mode of production. On this complex and important topic, I have learned a great deal from the rigorous and generous debate staged by two Johns Hopkins doctoral students, Benjamin Taylor and Rothin Datta.

Part I of the book strategically locates this thorny debate about the "origins" of capitalism within a larger account of the historical development of political economy. It therefore draws from (1) earlier debates within eighteenth- and nineteenth-century classical political economy, (2) theoretical work on the very nature of "history," and (3) contemporary writings in anthropology, history, and the history of economic ideas. The first group includes famous authors such as William Petty, François Quesnay, James Steuart, Adam Smith,

Jean-Baptiste Say, David Ricardo, James Mill, Samuel Bailey, and Karl Marx. The second group includes key theorists such as Friedrich Nietzsche, Michel Foucault, Timothy Mitchell, and Jairus Banaji. The final group ranges from Philip Mirowski to David Graeber to Angus Burgin.

Part II draws heavily from classical political economy and from readings of select authors in the neoclassical paradigm. And each chapter in Part II could quite easily become a book in itself. The theory and history of money proves to be a complicated, disputed, and at times vexed topic. Chapter 4 is therefore based on a deep reading of a wide range of literatures, and it draws from an extensive list of sources. This includes a more standard or "orthodox" reading of money as in its nature a commodity (Irving Fisher, William Stanley Jevons, and Carl Menger) contrasted with an alternative account of money as fundamentally a credit relation (R. G. Hawtrey, Henry Macleod, and A. Mitchell Innes). It draws from recent anthropological work, as represented by the lucid writings of David Graeber, who reveals barter to be a myth. And it reflects an engagement with the very best contemporary writers on money: Perry Mehrling, Geoffrey Ingham, and Randall Wray. Perhaps most significant of all is the one writer who does the best job of putting the complicated history of theories of money into a single picture, Joseph Schumpeter, who, unfortunately, does so only in an unfinished and posthumously published manuscript that runs to nearly 1300 pages in length and therefore will not make the below "recommended" list of further reading. In the near future I hope to fill this spot with a shorter and clearer book on money of my own (which does appear in the list).

Classical political economy emerges as a field of study *in ongoing response* to the emergence of a capitalist social order. And it is fair to say that across an enormous diversity of arguments and ideas, classical political economy focuses most intently on understanding one of the unique products of capitalism, the commodity. Hence Chapter 5 draws in a way from all of classical political economy, but especially from thinkers such as Petty, Smith, and Marx, who focused intensively on the twofold nature of a commodity as being *both* a use-value *and* an exchange-value. It was Marx, above all, who made this deeper ontological argument central to his analysis of the overall logic of capitalism. Marx tried to show that you could not make sense out of how capitalism works without linking the larger argument back to the commodity, which Marx famously called the "cell form" of capitalism—a metaphor meant to suggest that the best way of studying capitalism was to put the commodity under a microscope and then explore its significance across the entirety of a capitalist social order, which is just what this book tries to do. (The description of $xA = yB$ as "the impossible equation" in Chapter 5 is a phrase I have borrowed directly from Jacques Rancière.)

Chapter 6 poses a fundamental question that has been repeatedly forgotten over the course of the entire history of economic thought. At the end of the period of classical political economy, Marx argued that the primary limitation of the classical paradigm was its failure to truly explain the origin or source of profit. But soon after the consolidation of the neoclassical paradigm, the question of profit was again displaced (mainly because the neoclassical understanding of "equilibrium" led price to eclipse value). Key thinkers in the early twentieth century, especially Frank Knight, continued to explore the question of profit, but as the century wore on, this strand of Knight's work was lost to history (even as he himself was placed centrally as a founder of other strands of late twentieth-century economics). Marx's framework for posing the question of profit therefore still proves crucial today because it allows us to once again pose this frequently forgotten question.

Part III draws more heavily from the insights of Keynes and some of his best students, such as Hyman Minsky and particularly Joan Robinson. Like Schumpeter, Keynes viewed the functioning of a capitalist society through the eyes of the capitalist: a capitalist cycle of production can only begin with the choice of the entrepreneur to "advance capital." But less like Schumpeter, Keynes also recognized the fundamental importance of workers to the overall system. Without the availability of labor, capitalism cannot function, yet labor's availability is not a product of nature but rather a function of the overall capitalist system—of the social, political, and economic conditions under which the capitalist will advance capital. Therefore the entrepreneurial choice, the choice to properly *invest* in capitalist production, or merely to *save* value in the form of financial assets, becomes pivotal for the capitalist system. These core ideas also resonate with recent important arguments by today's most famous economist, Thomas Piketty, whose rigorous empirical work demonstrates something of the force of capital.

In turn, these insights also make the money markets central to our understanding of capitalist economics. Capitalism depends on access to liquidity, and dealers in money (whom we can roughly call "bankers") provide that liquidity. No one has done more to advance this argument than Perry Mehrling. In this way we see that Part III is not separate from or extraneous to Part I, with its focus on the primacy of production; to the contrary, there is a fundamental set of linkages between the money markets and the capitalist mode of production. Interest rates (and bond yield curves) often seem so opaque, or take on a kind of mythical status in explanations of political economy, precisely because a full understanding of something like interest rates requires tacking back and forth between money markets and production, with the circulation of commodities and money through exchange obviously mediating that circuit.

The "rules" of capitalism seek to express some of these higher-level connections that link all of the chapters of the book together. There are no direct sources for these rules themselves. However, the idea of rules that can themselves be broken, or that are understood only through their breaking, is a notion that can be traced throughout much of contemporary philosophy—from Ludwig Wittgenstein's "forms of life" to Michel Foucault's conception of "norms." On the one hand, some of the individual rules can be traced back to particular economic thinkers. On the other hand, the broader idea of explaining capitalist economics through "rules" of this type may be one of the unique contributions of this book, and if it takes inspiration from any prior source, it might be the fictional account of Star Trek's Ferengi species, the members of which explicitly articulated and lived by their own "rules of acquisition."

Further Reading

This section aims to provide a bit of guidance and orientation for those who have completed this work and wish to learn more—who want to engage more deeply in ideas traced here or who seek to explore new areas that this book just touches on. There is absolutely no single place to go next, no obvious place to continue the journey. The answer to the question of what to read next will depend on what the reader seeks. Therefore the texts listed here are not in any sort of linear order. Readers who have digested something of this book will be more than prepared to set out into any of the texts below, in whatever order they prefer. Nonetheless, because there are so many different places one might go, I have placed the following recommendations into groups.

For those interested in some of the historical texts, the following are suggested starting points. For classical political economy:

- David Ricardo, *Principles of Political Economy*, chapter 1, 1872 (30 pages)
- Karl Marx, "Value, Price and Profit," 1898 (lecture, 25 pages)

For work in the history of economic ideas that gives a broader overview of the emergence of the neoclassical paradigm and its break from classical political economy:

- Philip Mirowski, *More Heat Than Light*, 1989 (long book)

For those who want to go deeper into the conceptual and historical arguments about capitalism's "origins," the two places to begin are here:

- Ellen Meiksins Wood, *The Origin of Capitalism*, 2002 (short book)
- Jairus Banaji, *A Brief History of Commercial Capitalism*, 2020 (short book)

For those intrigued by the methodological and theoretical questions of locating *general* forces *within* history:

- Ellen Meiksins Wood, *Democracy Against Capitalism*, 1995 (book)
- Samuel Chambers, *Bearing Society in Mind*, 2013 (book)

For the recurring theme of Robinsonades, and the exploration of barter as a myth:

- Karl Marx, "1857 Introduction," 1973 (found in collections and in *Grundrisse*; 30 pages)
- David Graeber, "The Myth of Barter," chapter 2 of *Debt*, 2011 (20 pages)

For the best historical text on money, the best take on the broader "money view" of economics today, and a deeper exploration (historically and conceptually) of the nature of money, the following texts, respectively:

- A. Mitchell Innes, "What Is Money," in *Banking Law Journal*, 1913 (30 pages)
- Perry Mehrling, *The New Lombard Street*, 2011 (short book)
- Samuel Chambers, *Money Has No Value*, 2022 (book)

For the best introduction to the ideas of Keynes:

- Joan Robinson, *Introduction to the Theory of Employment*, 1969 (short book)

For an introduction to understanding Marx's work as a critique of classical political economy:

- Michael Heinrich, *An Introduction to the Three Volumes of Karl Marx's Capital*, 2004 (short book)

For a different approach to the idea of social orders and the economic force of capital:

- Thomas Piketty, *Capital and Ideology*, 2020 (long book)

For just the necessary foundational beginnings of an exploration of the deep entanglements between race and capitalism:

- W. E. B. Du Bois, *Black Reconstruction*, chapters 1 through 4, 1935 (100 pages)
- Eric Williams, *Capitalism and Slavery*, 1944 (book)
- Walter Rodney, *How Europe Underdeveloped Africa*, 1972 (long book)

Other Works Cited

Finally, the book specifically cites (parenthetically) a handful of works. Their full bibliographic details are provided here:

- Carter, Zachary. *The Price of Peace: Money, Democracy, and the Life of John Maynard Keynes*. New York: Random House, 2020.
- Ingham, Geoffrey. *The Nature of Money*. London: Polity, 2004.
- Innes, A. Mitchell. "The Credit Theory of Money." *Banking Law Journal*, 151: 151–68, 1914.
- Lanchester, John. "When Bitcoin Grows Up." *London Review of Books*, 38.8, 21 April 2016.
- McNally, David. *Monsters of the Market: Zombies, Vampires and Global Capitalism*. Leiden: Brill, 2011.
- Tarshis, Lorie. *Elements of Economics*. Cambridge, MA: The Riverside Press, 1947.

Acknowledgments

Nothing could be simpler than pointing out the severe limitations, blindspots, and fundamental errors in the teachings of current economics textbooks. But abandoning the abstract and simplified models of neoclassical economics and starting over poses a much sterner challenge. For many years I contemplated this feat from a distance, like a looming mountain summit that seems simply unscalable. I owe deep debts to so many people for helping me to contemplate and then supporting me in myriad ways as I tried to carry out this task.

I wrote Chapter 4 first, not as a chapter of a book, but strictly as an exercise—because I was compelled to develop an explanation of a fundamental economic phenomenon like money in a language that was clear and legible to anyone. Only after that chapter had come into the world did I dare to consider that a collection of such chapters could constitute a book, though at the time I was still not brave enough to write it. With her inspiring and enthusiastic response to a rough draft of the introduction, Angela Chnapko at Oxford University Press provided me with that courage. I thank Angela for her faith in the project and support of me throughout.

This book is dedicated to my students, and it owes its greatest debt to them as well. For more than a decade I have taught courses on capitalism at Johns Hopkins University. The excited engagement of students in my undergraduate seminars on "How to Be a Capitalist" spurred me to dig deeper into political economy and the history of economic thought. That research then became the basis for, and was further developed by, various graduate seminars on money, Marx, and political economy. Over the past two years I have taught early drafts of this book to two introductory undergraduate courses (in Spring 2020 and Spring 2021) and one graduate seminar (Fall 2020). I thank each and every student in those classes. I am particularly grateful to Felicia

Jing, Benjamin Taylor, and Darko Vinketa who, as TAs for those intro courses, themselves taught the book and helped me enormously to improve it. Ben both copyedited the manuscript and wrote the glossary of terms, thereby compounding the interest on my debt to him. Thanks go also to Rothin Datta and Henry Scott who both pushed forcefully on specific points in ways that the final product reflects.

Lester Spence and I co-taught a graduate seminar on "Racial Capitalism," a unique collaborative pedagogical experience from which I grew significantly as a scholar and teacher of capitalist economics. I am doubly indebted to Lester, because his own work on the nexus between neoliberal capitalism and Black politics is an exemplar of clarity and force toward which I aim. Alan Finlayson has long been a kind of compass for my research and writing, and he often proves to be my best reader. He provided an incisive set of criticisms of and suggestions for this project—and at just the right time. I continue to thank him. In terms of lucky timing, I was fortunate beyond belief that the Transnational Reading Group at Brighton University's Centre for Applied Philosophy, Politics and Ethics made a spur of the moment decision to read and discuss the manuscript of this book in April of 2020. The experience was incredibly helpful for me and I am profoundly grateful to all the participants, particularly Mark Devenney, Andy Knott, Rebecca Searle, and Clare Woodford.

For the past half-dozen years Paul Mariz and I have been engaged in a collaborative intellectual partnership that defies direct description, but central to that project has been an attempt to understand capitalism at the "quantum" level. Many of the basic arguments of this book I first rehearsed both in texts, slack posts, conversations, and especially in letters (yes, *letters*) to Paul. Paul has taught me more about science, coding, and music (just to name a few) than I have taught him about capitalism, but beyond this he also taught me something of how to teach capitalism—and that has been an invaluable resource for this book. I almost always find the English language excessive, in that it has more words to say the same thing than anyone could ever need. But English seems impoverished when it comes to saying thanks, which is why acknowledgments always bounce back and forth between the few terms available. To Paul, then, I say: Sega!

Rebecca Brown is the most gifted, dedicated, and accomplished teacher I know. As my partner, she is always my inspiration; in this project, she is also my aspiration. As always, the errors herein are mine; everything else I owe to Rebecca.

Glossary of Terms

(by Benjamin Taylor)

Arbitrage: A specific form of the capitalist use of markets in which commodities or securities are almost simultaneously bought in one market and sold in another in order to make a profit on pricing differentials. For early merchant capitalists, one source of profit was arbitrage in the form of "buying cheap and selling dear," only made possible by the fragmentation of markets separated by extended distances (though recent historical work has shown that this classic description of merchant capital does not adequately capture its manifold and varied relations with production).

Banks: Profit-maximizing firms that make money by making loans, an act that creates money endogenously within a capitalist economy. This new money appears on the banks' balance sheets as credits and debts: individuals and corporations hold deposit accounts (a liability for the bank) and loans (an asset for the bank).

$C \rightarrow C$: Formula representing the swap of one commodity for another; the exchange of equivalents. Trading in this way does not increase total value. It only moves around already produced, valuable commodities.

$C \rightarrow M \rightarrow C$: Formula representing the exchange of equivalents as mediated by money. Money in the sense of money of account (dollars, euros, etc.)— expressed in price—is the standard through which two commodities can be understood as equivalent, while money in the sense of an actual money credit is the vehicle by which one commodity is transformed into an equivalent commodity (money here mediates the transformation). Additionally, the introduction of money opens up the possibility that commodities are not exchanged immediately (such "bartering" has been rare across human history). This means that some people can sell goods purely in order to hoard money, and not to acquire other commodities immediately. This opens up the possibility of the capitalist use of markets.

ΔC : The change undergone in a capitalist production process from the initial commodity inputs (means of production and labor-power) to the final commodity product after production. ΔC denotes both the material distinction between C and C' and the mathematical difference in value between them. In order for the value of this final commodity (C') to be realized, it must be sold.

Capital: Capital is any element—money or commodities—within an active capitalist process of production. Any entity (commodity or money) actively taking on the role of M, C, C', or M' in that process is capital. Capital is not a thing, but a thing can be capital.

Capitalism: A social order that is organized, structured, and maintained by and through a capitalist mode of production, which is to say a mode of production where production is oriented toward profit in the form of money. A capitalist mode of production is characterized by the following formula: $M \rightarrow C...P...C' \rightarrow M'$

Capitalist Economics: The shape that decisions about production, consumption, distribution, and exchange take in a social order characterized by a capitalist mode of production. By distinguishing between capitalism and economics, we are emphasizing that economic forces are different in different types of social orders.

Capitalist Use of Markets: The use of markets to make money rather than to exchange equivalents. This use is made possible by the intervention of money in exchange processes ($C \rightarrow M \rightarrow C$ rather than $C \rightarrow C$).

Capitalists: Those who live not by selling their labor-power but by using M to achieve M'. Capitalists may be entrepreneurs, bankers, or merchants. Capitalist production could not take place if entrepreneurs did not advance money capital (the initial M in the capitalist code). Entrepreneurs themselves can often only access that money capital by borrowing it from bankers for a fee (interest). Finally, many powerful firms, both historically and currently, profit primarily by "making markets": buying commodities from producers at one price and then selling them at a higher price. Modern-day examples of merchant capital include Walmart and Amazon.

Causal Linear Explanation: A method of explanation presupposing that changes in the dependent variable are the effect of exogenous changes in the independent variable. Its basic form is "A causes B." Such causes can be positive (A and B change in the same direction) or negative (A and B move in opposite directions). Most modern economics depends on the effort to isolate independent variables that have the strongest causal force producing determinate outcomes.

Central Banks: Banks for bankers. Commercial banks have their own form of deposit account with the central bank (in the form of central bank reserves) and their own form of loans (reserves borrowed from the central bank). When one individual pays another with bank deposits (checks or direct transfer), their banks must also transfer central bank reserves. The central bank is the "lender of last resort" in a capitalist society. It can backstop otherwise failing financial institutions because it need not be concerned with profits or losses in the same way that commercial banks are. Finally, by setting and altering the central bank lending rate, the central bank can indirectly influence interbank lending rates (and thus also interest rates throughout the rest of the economy). We have described central banks as the "cardiologists" of capitalism.

Class Relations: The social, legal, and political relationships that characterize a given mode of production. Each social order develops a distinct set of patterns and connections between relations of production and broader categories of power and identity. Production under capitalism is distinguished by the widespread sale and purchase of labor-power from wage laborers: people who must rent out their time in order to earn the money needed to purchase the necessaries of life. Feudalism, on the other hand, typically involves the direct legal appropriation (by the church and by feudal lords) of some portion of serfs' production. Other modes of production include peasant production, in which small family groups produce largely for their own consumption, with surplus appropriated directly by the state. Understanding a mode of production requires us to grasp the class relations that characterize it. However, a mode of production is not reducible to the way in which labor is managed and its fruits appropriated because every social order has a variety of complex social, legal, and property relations that also help to determine the overall nature of that society.

Classical Political Economy: The field that studied economic forces in relation to political forces from the seventeenth century through the late nineteenth century. Major authors in classical political economy include James Steuart, William Petty, Adam Smith, David Ricardo, and J. B. Say. For more authors, see the "Sources and Further Reading" section of this book.

Commodity: A useful thing produced in order to be sold. The fullest development of the commodity only occurs within a capitalist mode of production, where production is oriented to exchange. A capitalist commodity is metaphysically dual: it *is* both a use-value and an exchange-value.

Credit: That which can redeem a debt; a specific denominated claim held by one party on or against another party.

Derivatives: A type of contract between two parties wherein the price of the derivative itself depends on—and changes according to changes in—the price of some separate "underlying" financial asset. When money-market dealers or bankers create a derivative, they give actors in money markets the ability to bet for or against an underlying asset without actually owning it.

Economic: Distinct from "economics," an academic discipline that studies the sum of individual choices as either realizing or failing to realize the "efficient allocation of scarce resources." "Economic" is an adjective that modifies various nouns and emphasizes how specific types of forces work to constitute and characterize real-world events.

Efficiency: A concept borrowed by late nineteenth-century neoclassical economics from the discipline of physics, where it had originally measured energy output/energy input. Economists often argue that capitalism is the most "efficient" economic system or that free markets are the most "efficient" distributors of resources, but these claims make little sense given the definition of *efficiency*, which these analysts implicitly confuse with *optimality*. Finally, whether and how capitalist firms seek to maximize efficiency in production is subordinate to the drive to increase profits. Sometimes, firms in certain industries will intentionally refrain from maximizing output in order to restrict supply and keep profits high.

Entrepreneur: A capitalist enterprise owner. Someone with access to money who invests it—that is, someone who buys labor-power and means of production in order to begin a capitalist production process.

Equivalents: Two distinct goods posited as equal (at a given ratio) through exchange. Money/price is the standard through which their equality can be judged.

Exchange-Value: The value of a commodity as expressed in a ratio with some other commodity or commodities, or the price of the commodity (as posited in money). The realization of exchange-value in the form of money is the aim of capitalist production.

Good: A good is a resource that has been appropriated in some process of production. Under capitalism, "goods" take the form of commodities: useful things produced for the sake of sale.

Historical Contingency: An element of this book's approach emphasizing that economic "laws" are only valid for given historical periods. Every such "law" expresses its force only on the basis of institutional and systemic patterns of organization that make it possible. This approach thus foregrounds those patterns and institutions in order to see how what appear to be "laws" are often closer to "rules," which can be, and sometimes are, broken.

Impossible Equation: $xA = yB$. Through exchange, nonidentical objects are made equal with each other. Under capitalism, exchange prices become regularized through market-maker competition, so the many and varied manifestations of this equation take on a degree of stability.

Inequality: Inequality is required by capitalism. Some people must be workers, whereas others have access to flows of money or means of production and therefore do not have to work for a living. If everyone were an entrepreneur, capitalist production could not take place.

Interest: A charge or fee demanded by the holder of money (banks or other private creditors) of a person seeking access to that money (who thereby becomes a debtor). There is no single interest rate. Rather, different rates of interest reflect relations of power in a given society (i.e., who can demand how much before you can access money?).

Investment: An action undertaken by entrepreneurs to purchase the raw materials, means of production, and labor-power needed to undertake capitalist production.

Labor-power: Not simply the generic capacity to labor but rather the unique shape the capacity to labor takes under capitalism, where it is given the form of a commodity through the wage contract. Capitalist production depends on the short-term sale of labor-power. Because of the special nature of the wage relation—the entrepreneur pays less for labor-power than the value the labor of the worker generates during the production process—labor-power can serve the role of profit commodity and is consequently the source of all surplus value.

$M \rightarrow C \rightarrow M'$: The formula for the capitalist use of markets. Money is used to purchase commodities, which are in turn sold for more money. This was typically only possible because markets were disconnected, so merchants would purchase goods cheaply in one place, transport them, and sell them more expensively in another.

$M \rightarrow C...P...C' \rightarrow M'$: The formula for capitalist production. Money is used to purchase commodities (means of production and labor-power), which are then used up in a capitalist production process that generates new commodities. These commodities must then be sold in order to realize their value, and doing so permits capitalists to make a profit.

ΔM : Change in M that takes place between the money invested at the start of production and the money obtained through the sale of commodities at the end (the difference between M and M'). From the perspective of the entrepreneur, ΔM is nothing more than accounting profit, but from the perspective of the student of capitalist economics, ΔM represents and presupposes the production of surplus value.

Marginalist Revolution: During the 1870s three different scholars with backgrounds mostly in mathematics and engineering, William Stanley Jevons, Karl Menger, and Léon Walras, attempted to break with the tradition of classical political economy by using the language of mathematics and the metaphors of physics to create new models of economics as a science. Retroactively, this body of work became known as the marginalist "revolution" because each author was thought to have independently "discovered" the idea of diminishing marginal utility. The marginalist revolution therefore marks the break between classical political economy and the neoclassical paradigm.

Markets: A space—whether immediately physical or nonlocal (e.g., digital, via newspaper, over the phone, etc.)—where commodities are bought and sold. Markets require "market makers" to operate: people who have a store of both money and commodities, and who will purchase commodities of a certain type at one price and sell them at another, higher price. Early merchant capitalists, themselves market makers of a sort, helped to develop the world market, on which the emergence and continued existence of a capitalist mode of production depend, though market makers have not become any less central since the capitalist use of markets has become a mere moment of a capitalist mode of production rather than an independent technique of profit-seeking.

Means of Production: The basic materials required for production. Under capitalism, these must be purchased as commodities. Means of production (*MP*) include both raw materials completely used up in the production process *and* tools and machinery that wear out over time.

Merchant Capitalism: A historical period dating from roughly the twelfth through fourteenth centuries, marked distinctively by the capitalist use of markets. Recent historical work has demonstrated how merchants would use numerous techniques to dominate preindustrial production in order to guarantee and increase their profits. The capitalist imperative constantly to revolutionize the production process was especially present for merchant capitalists in the realm of transportation (for example, see the history of Dutch shipping improvements). Also called "commercial capitalism."

Mode of Production: The broad structures, systems, techniques, and practices that create overall societal output. The overall "system of production" and "the process of production" are both synonyms for "mode of production."

Money Capital: Value in its money form when it has been put in motion in a capitalist production process. It can either be spent directly on the initial C (MP and LP) required for a capitalist production process or can be lent out to entrepreneurs who then spend it in this manner.

Money: Money is a "first-class credit." To have money means to have a credit with some other entity that recognizes that credit as their debt. Money is always an asset for one person and a liability for someone else. A completed money transaction always involves at least three parties: buyer, seller (who receives credits), and debtor (individual or institution on which those credits are held).

Neoclassical Paradigm of Economics: This account of economics displaced classical political economy through the "marginalist revolution" of the 1870s. It was during this time that those studying economic forces posited "general equilibrium" as a state the economy could reach and also adopted *efficiency* as the main term to characterize economics. The neoclassical paradigm has been the dominant paradigm of modern economics for over a century.

Net Revenue: A given firm's accounting profit—that is, total cash inflows over a given period less total cash outflows. Net revenue is always derived from the overall production of surplus value, but merely accounting for a specific firm's profit does not explain where surplus value comes from at a systemic level.

Optimality: Optimality concerns the best distribution of resources in a society. Economists sometimes confuse optimality with the narrower, technical question of efficiency. However, the question of the "best distribution of resources" cannot be answered on purely technical grounds because it involves broader social, political, and moral concerns.

Political Economy: The study of economics and politics not as discrete areas of social life but as different types of forces that interact with each other in complex ways. Political economy does not take economic forces to be natural and timeless but rather understands them as manifesting differently across different historical periods and social orders. Thus it is more attentive to the historical status of economic "rules," including those that characterize capitalism.

Power: Michel Foucault famously described power as the "conduct of conduct": the ability to influence how others act. While power is expressed in many ways in contemporary society, including through the systems of meaning by which we seek to apprehend the world, the most ubiquitous form under capitalism is money. If you don't have access to flows of money, your options for action are extremely limited. Money, rather than a neutral veil for the exchange of commodities, is a form of political control without any specific controller or operator, though it is ultimately backed up by the threat of force (from creditors or their agents).

Price: The ideal expression of value as quantified in some unit of account (dollars, euros, beaver pelts, etc.). These units of account are highly variable and emerge from distinct patterns of historical development.

Primacy of Production: While the neoclassical paradigm takes exchange as its primary concern, we focus instead on the different ways that societies produce—with respect not only to their levels of technical development but also to the social relations that characterize their production processes. For example, while production under feudalism was largely undertaken by serfs who were legally bonded to lords and forced to work on lords' estates, production under capitalism is generally characterized by the "formal freedom" of waged workers, who must voluntarily contract with capitalists in order to acquire the money necessary for their survival. Further, while production under feudalism was oriented toward private consumption, production under capitalism is oriented toward the constant expansion of value/money via the sale of commodities for profit. By focusing on exchange instead of production, the neoclassical paradigm emphasizes an element common to many modes of production (i.e., markets for the exchange of goods and services) rather than what makes a mode of production unique (the purpose of production and the social relations that characterize it).

Production/Distribution/Exchange/Consumption: Ostensibly the four main concerns of both classical political economy and the neoclassical paradigm. However, distribution and consumption largely fall out of analysis. Further, under the neoclassical paradigm, production is studied as if it were isomorphic with exchange: "society" is treated as a single consumer deciding between already established production options. However, this is not how production under capitalism actually takes place. Rather, private producers seek to maximize profit, and they engage in fierce competition to achieve the highest possible rates of return to capital. Part of capitalist competition involves the constant revolutionizing of the production process.

Productivity: Total output of commodities manufactured during a given number of labor-hours. Not to be confused with the *profit* achieved from a given number of labor-hours. Increased productivity tends to *decrease* the price of any given commodity by decreasing the amount of labor-power it takes to produce an article. Improvements in machine technology or the organization of labor processes are the main ways that capitalist firms increase their productivity.

Profit Commodity: A commodity whose use generates more value than its own exchange-value. Only labor-power can function as the profit commodity because of the unique nature of the wage relation (i.e., labor-power costs less to buy than the value labor-power generates in production). While the relationship between a waged proletariat and large-scale factory production is one of capitalism's most apparent and historically novel features, especially in its early industrial period, labor-power's subordination to capital has taken (and takes) a variety of different forms (including, perhaps most notably, New World slavery).

Profit: The "cut" of overall surplus value (as created through global capitalist production) that shows up on the spreadsheets of entrepreneurs after they have paid out rents to bankers and landlords (who will in turn book those rents as profits on their spreadsheets).

Quantity Theorem of Money: A theorem stating that when the overall "supply" of money goes up, its "price" (i.e., purchasing power) will necessarily decrease. Not only has this theorem been proven entirely false, most recently by quantitative easing as a reaction to the 2008 recession, it treats money as if it were a commodity. In reality, money is not a commodity; it is a social relation of transferable credit/debt. Prices increase due to prior shifts in the supply of and demand for given commodities. These movements, especially on the supply side, take place on the basis of capitalist firms' production decisions, which they make while seeking to maximize profit.

Raw Materials: Inputs for production processes. They are a component of the initial C in the code for capitalist production. In this sense, raw materials are not merely found in nature but are rather the effect of appropriation through some production process (and appropriation from nature's reserves is itself a process of "production").

Rent: Rent is not capital, nor is it surplus value. Rent is a cost that precedes an entrepreneur's initial C. It is a cost of doing business that capitalist property relations, specifically private property in land, permit some people (landlords) to extract from others (those in need of space in which to carry out production). Rent is paid out of surplus value and appears to landlords as accounting profit.

Resources: The various existing things that can be usefully used by humans, including air, water, land, food, materials for shelter, energy sources, and so forth. These are not immediately economic goods but only become so when they are appropriated as part of a specific process of production and distribution.

Risk: Risk is unavoidable under capitalism; there is no risk-free way to maintain value. Inflation (or even the failure of an entire monetary system) can erode the purchasing power of money. Commodities might fail to sell. Financial assets might lose value overnight as the result of other transformations in the economy. As such, the prevailing view that those with money must be appeased lest they flee with their money to riskless havens is a myth. Rather, the question is how to encourage the socially optimal use of money in the face of ineliminable risk.

Robinsonade: The name given to a genre of literary tale that began in the seventeenth century and flourished after the publication of Daniel Defoe's *Robinson Crusoe*. Such stories portray some individual (or group of individuals) becoming outcast from developed society and seeking to recreate its conditions on their own. Robinsonades make contemporary societies seem necessary by naturalizing the tendencies, mores, norms, and so on, that are present within them. Much of mainstream economic analysis works within the Robinsonade genre, but proper studies of capitalist economics must operate as anti-Robinsonades, asking how capitalist societies developed historically rather than treating them as natural or timeless.

Rules of Capitalism: The general and necessary tendencies that characterize production in a capitalist social order. These are sometimes broken but nevertheless generally hold true. These rules are:

1. Money must beget more money.
   1a. Money is the means of survival.
2. Markets regulate prices.
3. Producers must produce profitable commodities.
4. Technological change and "innovation" are required (not optional).
5. Crisis is unavoidable.

Saving: The purchase of stocks, bonds, or other financial assets. An action undertaken in lieu of investment when rates of return on financial assets are higher than expected returns to capital investment.

Scarcity: A term indicating that there is not enough of a commodity relative to demand. "Scarce" is a term that consequently only ever applies within a society. It is contrasted with "limited," a term designating that resources are finite (which applies to everything inside and outside of society).

Security: A financial instrument (i.e., a form of money-credit) that can be divided into the following categories: equities (i.e., stocks), debts (e.g., certificates of deposit, bonds), and derivatives. Buying securities is not capitalist investment. Rather, it is a form of saving.

Social Orders: Different forms of society at various degrees of scale (e.g., tribes, villages, cities, nations, empires). Every social order is historically specific, and each is made up of a variety of forces, relations, and logics—including political, social, cultural, and economic forces.

Surplus Value: Surplus value is a system-level result achieved in a capitalist social order. It describes the total increase in money/value that results from overall capitalist production. This can be understood as the difference between C and C', or it can be grasped as the system-wide ΔM that captures the difference between M' and M. Surplus value is generated in the process of production. While it serves as the basis for all profit, it is not itself simply identical to profit. The profits of individual firms, entrepreneurs, or merchants are instead a *cut* of overall surplus value. Recognizing that surplus value is generated in production explains how capitalist economies grow despite goods and services being bought and sold at their values.

Twofold Nature: This term describes the character of capitalist commodities. Capitalist commodities do not *have* both a use-value and an exchange-value but rather *are* both use-values and exchange-values (i.e., useful things that people want to buy). Whether a good is an exchange-value depends on whether it can satisfy a given social need of whatever type, which in turn requires it to be a use-value.

Use-Value: The direct, physical existence of a good or product that makes it intrinsically useful, regardless of whether any person has an immediate need for the good.

Value: Value under capitalism takes the form of money (and price is value posited in money terms). Value is essential to capitalism as a social order that produces commodities, which are twofold entities (use-value and exchange-value), in order to sell those commodities for money profit (M'). Capital is "value in motion," and this means that commodities and means of production are only moments of value to the extent that they are actively involved in capitalist production or are circulating as commodity capital. While it is created in production, value is only ever realized in sale. When anything playing the role of capital exits the capitalist process of production—workers go home, products are sold, machines are taken offline—it ceases to be capital.

Vascular Metaphor: Capitalism is a giant system that circulates money and commodities in exchange for one another. Throughout the book, we have compared this system to the actual working of the body's cardiovascular system. The following terms have been deployed:

- money = blood plasma [the liquid force that carries commodities along]
- commodities = blood cells [circulating elements characterized by a static form, a cellular structure]
- money + commodities = blood [the substance that constantly circulates]
- production = heart [production under capitalism is like an imaginary heart that constantly generates an ever-expanding amount of blood; it is required to keep money and commodities circulating, especially since commodities are constantly consumed, both productively and unproductively]
- interest rates = pulse [a measure of how circulation is taking place; are money and commodities circulating at a high rate, or has the rate of return slowed down such that "saving" seems like a better option for those with money?]
- entrepreneurs = pacemaker (ICD) [those who jumpstart the production process]
- central bank = cardiologist [the institution that manipulates the interest rate for commercial bank borrowing, i.e., capitalism's most important "pulse," thereby altering the rate of flow of production]

Workers: Under capitalism, the members of a society who must sell their time as labor-power in order to survive. They are essential to the production process. Capitalist production could not take place if there were not large numbers of people who have to act as workers, contrary to myths supposing everyone could be an entrepreneur.